Your Towns and Cities in the Gɪ

Oswestry and Whitchurch
in the Great War

Contents

	Acknowledgements	6
	Introduction	7
1	1913 Before the Conflict	9
2	1914 And so it begins...	23
3	1914 The Effect at Home	30
4	Shropshire's Main Military Camps	47
5	1915 U-Boats and Zeppelins	64
6	1916 The Year of the Somme	83
7	1917 The War Intensifies	108
8	Oswestry and Whitchurch Heroes	129
9	1918 And so it ends...	140
10	1919 The Aftermath	155
	Bibliography	171
	Index	172

Acknowledgements

I have endeavoured to verify all the facts used in this book which have been gathered using available archive material, printed information and various websites. All pictures and photographs used have been credited wherever possible and any omissions are unintentional.

I would particularly like to thank the staff and volunteers at both Oswestry and Whitchurch libraries who couldn't have been more helpful, Peter Lea at the Raven Café, Prees Heath whose knowledge of the camp which once existed there is inexhaustible, Keith and Kath Griffiths from Whittington for allowing me use of their material, the staff at Pen and Sword for their support, and last but not least my husband Bob (1942–2016), who encouraged me throughout the project as well as producing photographs for the publication and to whom I dedicate this book.

If I have inadvertently omitted anyone from the above please accept my apologies.

Jan Johnstone
September 2015

Introduction

Much has been written of the First World War: the awful conditions soldiers had to endure in a conflict that saw the first use of tanks and poison gas; the millions of civilians who lost their lives worldwide, allies and enemy alike; the devastated battlegrounds riddled with shell holes and muddy trenches alive with vermin; the silence when the constant bombardment ceased, for there were no birds left to sing. . . all this needs to be remembered.

In this book, however, I have tried to show how the First World War impacted on the lives of people living in two thriving market towns in north Shropshire – Oswestry and Whitchurch. Although the towns did not have to endure the bombing that more industrialised British towns and cities went through, nevertheless they had to learn to adapt to many changes in their everyday routine. The rules and regulations that were introduced, some of which led to much hardship as the war progressed, the tremendous effort that went into fundraising for a wide variety of causes, the provision and staffing of auxiliary hospitals created to deal with the wounded, the influx of hundreds of soldiers from newly created camps adjacent to the towns; all had a profound effect on daily life.

It's clear that over past centuries both towns had been subjected to turbulent and violent times, ownership passing frequently between the warring factions of England and Wales. As a result, communities had seen their homes burnt to the ground only to rise again with fresh masters as new invaders arrived. There is little doubt that an inherited urge to defend land, property and loved ones was inbuilt in the character of people living in both Oswestry and Whitchurch prior to 1914. So when Britain's intention to go to war with Germany was announced on 4 August 1914 and an urgent call to arms went out for volunteers, the young men of Oswestry, Whitchurch and surrounding districts came forward promptly, leaving behind them anxious families who nevertheless were proud to see them march away to defend their king, their country and their way of life.

CHAPTER 1

1913
Before the Conflict

❖

In 1913 Britain was experiencing one of the best summers in living memory; it had its vast Empire, was a powerful and influential figure in the world with new industrial innovations reported on daily, whilst British explorers went to extremes to set new records of bravery and daring, returning home as heroes. In the two Shropshire towns of Oswestry and Whitchurch life carried on much the same as usual with its newspapers either shocking or enthralling readers with their content. In February news that Captain Scott's expedition to the South Pole had been a failure was met with dismay, whilst in April headlines announcing that Emmeline Pankhurst, the suffragette, had been sentenced to three years penal servitude received a decidedly mixed reception depending on the reader's opinions.

In May the Black Country Strike saw 40,000 workers, who sought equal pay with those employed in similar trades in Birmingham, brought out on strike by their unions which lasted until July 1913. Continuing to dominate Parliamentary debate and headlines in July and August were Ireland's demands for Home Rule, whilst on a lighter note widely reported on was Bernard Shaw's play 'Pygmalion' which had outraged members of the audience on its first night by including the phrase 'not bloody likely' in its dialogue.

But the rumbles of discontent that had been slowly building up overseas were increasing to a roar with tensions running dangerously high. European powers were experiencing increasing political, territorial and economic conflict between their borders and something had to give.

A history of Oswestry
The first sign of occupation near the town of Oswestry occurred in 600BC when Iron Age tribesmen began the construction of a hill fort later known as Caer Ogyrfan. The fort covered fifty-six acres and over the years numerous ramparts and ditches were added to it. Here, legend has it, Queen Guinevere was born. In August AD642 not far from the fort, King Oswald of Northumbria and his army were battling pagan King Penda of Mercia and his Welsh allies for ownership of the area. Oswald was slain at the hands of Penda who decreed that to further demoralise an army which had suffered a devastating defeat, Oswald's body be dismembered with the head, arms and hands displayed on wooden stakes on the battlefield. Legend has it that a raven swooped down and, seizing the dead king's right arm, carried it up into an ash tree before dropping it back to the ground. Where it landed a spring burst forth, later becoming a place of pilgrimage for Oswald's followers who believed the water had healing qualities.

By the time of the Norman occupation William the Conqueror had given the region to his trusted follower Roger de Montgomery, a somewhat dubious honour as the Domesday Book recorded the area as a wasteland, ravaged by Anglo-Welsh rebellions. He, in turn, passed ownership to Rainald de Bailleul, Sheriff of Shropshire and the builder of Oswestry's castle. From then on the town and the surrounding lands saw frequent changes of both fortune and ownership.

By 1407 Oswestry had its own grammar school, founded by David Holbache, an innovative local landowner, lawyer and politician. The school taught Latin, Greek and English grammar as well as longbow skills required by law at the time. In 1577 Queen Elizabeth I endowed the school *'of her Mercy with forty shillings yearly toward the maytenance of the Said school'* to help with its upkeep. Later, during the English Civil War, the school came under the stern eye of Oliver Cromwell who promptly dismissed the headmaster, not won over by Parliamentarian beliefs, peevishly declaring him 'too delinquent'.

The castle was in use as a military stronghold during the English Civil War, Oswestry supporting the Royalists. It was finally taken by

St Oswald's Well off Maserfield Road, Oswestry. Records show that in 1881 the feeble and infirm still visited to bathe in the well's healing waters.

The Old Grammar School established in 1407, St Oswald's Church in the background.

All that remains of Oswestry's Castle today. (Bob Johnstone)

the Parliamentarians on 22 June 1644 when the town's gates were breached and the town capitulated. To prevent the Royalists re-taking the castle Oliver Cromwell ordered it razed to the ground in 1647 and much of the rubble was used in buildings around the growing town.

With the arrival of the Industrial Revolution Oswestry was expanding rapidly. Particularly important were the railways coming into the very heart of the town. Agriculture, long a mainstay of the area, was changing too, with fresh methods of farming being introduced and by the end of the nineteenth century Oswestry's population had doubled from 5,500 in 1861 to nearly 10,000 at the beginning of the 1900s, helped considerably by the arrival of the Cambrian Railway headquarters and workshops in 1865.

Cambrian Railway Headquarters today. (Bob Johnstone)

Oswestry in 1913

By 1913 Oswestry was able to offer good transport links, with roads, railways and canals all providing an essential service for the town and boroughs in the vicinity. Its Guildhall, built in 1893 on Bailey Head in a style described as seventeenth century renaissance, housed the council offices and the county court as well as police cells, a free public library and reading rooms. Oswestry had its own gas, water and electric light works, a police station and a fire station. A main post office and two sub-post offices opened seven days a week and the town had plenty of shops. A newspaper, the *Oswestry & Border Counties Advertizer*, published weekly, kept its readers up to date with both local and world events, as it still does today.

Oswestry Territorials, B Squadron, Shropshire Yeomanry and H Company, the 4th Battalion of the King's Shropshire Light Infantry, met in the Drill Hall and had been founded in 1907 when the Yeomanry joined up with the Volunteer Force.

A cinematograph theatre, several public halls and theatres all hosted a range of events to entertain throughout the year. Oswestry had at least thirty-three public houses and beer houses, popular with thirsty farmers on market days, while a corporation gymnasium and swimming baths encouraged more healthy pursuits. Cae Glas Park, eight acres of land formerly the grounds of a large mansion demolished in 1835, were purchased in 1909 by the Corporation for £6,000. Gardens were laid out and a bandstand with regular concerts provided a popular spot for the locals to gather.

A grammar school for boys adjacent to St Oswald's Church, a girls' high school and public elementary schools for mixed classes and infants saw to the education of local children, these supplemented further by church schools and a number of private schools.

The townspeople's wellbeing was taken care of by the Oswestry Provident Dispensary, Victoria Street, where for a small weekly payment, treatment was available for out-patients. Oswestry and Ellesmere Cottage Hospital and Nursing Association on Welsh Walls catered for more serious cases.

St Oswald's Parish Church together with churches of other denominations looked after spiritual needs and were well-attended. All would be needed in the years to come providing comfort for the bereaved.

Smales Almshouses housed six married couples, each entitled to a bequest of £3 per year, with residents chosen and houses kept in good repair by Lord Harlech from nearby Brogyntyn Hall. An important figure in the town, he and his wife Margaret supported the community in a variety of ways.

Malting, tanning, foundries, agricultural implement making, machine works and steam sawmills, with coal mining, limestone

St Oswald's Parish Church, Oswestry.

quarrying and brick making taking place in nearby parishes, all provided ample employment. The Cambrian Railway Company Engine and Carriage Works employed a workforce of 1,900 in 1913.

Agriculture was an immensely important part of the local economy with regular markets for the sale of both produce and animals, the Cross Market selling meat, fish, greengrocery, poultry and general produce twice weekly on Wednesdays and Saturdays. A wholesale cheese and butter fair also took place in the Powis Market, Bailey Head on the first Wednesday of every month.

Railway transport to and from the town had begun with the arrival of the Shrewsbury and Chester Railway in 1848, taken over by the Great Western Railway (GWR) in 1854. By 1866 the Cambrian Railway main line from Whitchurch to Aberystwyth was established and local omnibuses met every train to convey passengers into the town.

A history of Whitchurch
Whitchurch, situated on the old Roman Road of Watling Street, midway between the settlements of Viroconium (Wroxeter), and Deva (Chester) is claimed to be the oldest continuously inhabited community in north Shropshire. It owes its origins to a Roman military fort, Mediolanum, the 'place in the middle of the plain' built in 43 AD and by the time the fort was abandoned a township had begun to establish itself. There followed centuries of changes of ownership, including in 650 AD occupation by the Saxons who re-named the settlement Westune (West Farmstead).

In 1066 William the Conqueror gave Whitchurch to William de Warenne who built a motte and bailey there in 1100. At the same time he also replaced the old Saxon church with one of white Grinshill stone taken from a local quarry. The church quickly gained the name 'Album Monasterium' or White Church, leading in time to the name Whitchurch. Granted town status by Edward I in 1284, Whitchurch grew rapidly; it was not safe from raids from over the border, however, suffering frequent invasions by the Welsh. A particularly devastating attack took place in 1404 when the town was burnt to the ground. It took seven long years to rebuild.

As with many Shropshire towns during the Civil War, Whitchurch declared itself a Royalist stronghold and in 1642 Royalist Lord Capel set out from nearby Prees Heath, some three miles from Whitchurch, with a large contingent of men, cannons and field guns to storm the Parliamentarian town of Wem, some ten miles distant, on the king's behalf. Stopped in his tracks by just forty soldiers and the women of the town, a humiliating rhyme was soon circulating detailing his failure, *'the women of Wem and a few musketeers, beat Lord Capel and all his cavaliers'*.

During the following centuries Whitchurch continued to expand with a new church built in 1713 of red and grey sandstone in neo-classical style to replace the fifteenth century medieval building which had collapsed.

St Alkmund's Parish Church, Whitchurch.

By 1808, a branch from the nearby Ellesmere canal terminating in two wharves at Sherryman's Bridge had been constructed and three years later further works, consisting of a landing stage and canal warehouses, were built where the town mill, by now derelict, had stood.

A station had been established by 1858 on the Crewe to Shrewsbury

Drawbridge on the Canal, Whitchurch

The Shropshire Union Canal once led into the centre of town.

Whitchurch

railway line improving transport and bringing into the town not only goods, but also more people, providing trade for its shops and markets.

Whitchurch in 1913
In 1913 the Urban and Rural District Councils took care of both Whitchurch and its outlying hamlets meeting in the Town Hall, a red-brick building with white stone facings built in 1872 at a cost of £3,000. As well as Council Chambers, the Town Hall housed Assembly Rooms, a Corn Exchange and a weekly general market.

Whitchurch had gas and waterworks to supply it but no electricity, this was finally installed in the 1930s. A police station in Green End manned by a superintendent, a sergeant and four constables, together with two fire brigades, one in Brownlow Street, the other in St Mary's Street, ensured the safety of local inhabitants.

B Company of the 4th Battalion of the King's Shropshire Light Infantry met in Egerton Drill Hall in New Street, whilst Melton Lodge, an imposing red brick building, housed the headquarters of the Mounted Brigade Field Ambulance Army Medical Corps, a mobile front line medical unit.

The *Whitchurch Herald* in High Street published a weekly newspaper which is still in production today, whilst a wide variety of shops plus twenty public houses supplied other needs. The Working Men's Hall on Castle Hill contained a library, club, reading room, classrooms and a concert room and was also used for the county court and magistrates' meetings. The town also had a public baths, built at a cost of £1,500 in 1891, whilst the Whitchurch Institute above the Town Hall provided other recreational facilities.

A free library, museum and picture gallery in the High Street was donated to Whitchurch people by Mr E.P. Thompson, a local benefactor, and Jubilee Park on the western side of the town, bought by public subscription to commemorate Queen Victoria's Jubilee, provided eleven acres of grounds for all to enjoy.

A grammar school built in 1848 replaced an older building in Bargates with a high school for girls and public elementary and infants schools taking care of the education of local children.

Whitchurch Cottage Hospital and Dispensary, housed in a half-timbered building in Brownlow Street, had its own operating facilities,

The Cottage Hospital and Dispensary, Whitchurch.

whilst an isolation hospital located at nearby Prees Heath, dealt with outbreaks of infectious diseases.

Almshouses in Bargates, erected in 1697 through a bequest by Samuel Higginson and added to in 1708 by his wife Jane, housed the needy whilst further almshouses were built in 1829 by benefactress Elizabeth Langford in Dodington High Street. The occupants, referred to as *'indigent and decayed men or women inhabitants in the parish of Whitchurch and members of the established Church of England'* were obliged to attend church every Sunday unless there was a very good reason why they couldn't.

The Church of St Alkmund, constructed in Classic style in 1713, stood at the top of Whitchurch High Street with other places of worship, including Baptist, Primitive Methodist, Wesleyan Methodist and Unitarian Churches were spread around the town.

Brewing, malting, agriculture, tanning and, in particular, cheese making, provided a living, but the biggest employer in the town was W.H. Smith and Company, Engineering and Ironfounders, who produced farm implements, structural ironwork, cheese vats and dairy equipment. Wyatt Brothers, established 1879, manufactured water heating equipment for use in steam dairies and agriculture; very well-known locally were the long-established turret clock-makers J.B. Joyce whose products were famous throughout the world.

Markets took place every Friday selling cattle, corn, butter and meat whilst a highly successful and extremely well known cheese fair was held every third Wednesday. A railway station, built in 1858, encouraged people to visit Whitchurch whilst the Ellesmere Canal was extensively used, providing a passenger service daily with narrowboats

J.B. Joyce, world-renowned clock-makers. Today the building is an auctioneers. (Bob Johnstone)

leaving the town wharf for Ellesmere Port in Cheshire from where it was possible to travel to Liverpool, Birmingham or the Potteries. The canal was also used to transport coal, lime and iron whilst cheeses were transported in specially equipped narrowboats known as Cheese Flys to Manchester markets or the port of Liverpool for eventual export. Boots, leather goods and other local products were also carried on the canal.

Very few going about their busy everyday lives in Oswestry and Whitchurch probably took much note of what was happening abroad as the end of the year approached, and those that did read of the problems in the Balkans in their local newspaper would most probably have turned to more local issues, dismissing the reports as far away and nothing to do with Britain.

On the last day of December 1913, as the minutes counted down towards midnight and the bells of St Oswald's and St Alkmund's rang out in their respective towns, cheering crowds took to the streets to celebrate. Of those gathered together none could have possibly imagined just how much life was going to change for all of them over the next four years.

New Year 1914 was nearly here and that summer, an incident would take place in Europe that would ignite the bloodiest conflict the world had ever know, an event which would also, in the years to come, lead to life-changing events for everyone.

CHAPTER 2

1914
And so it begins...

❖

On 28 June 1914 at 9.28am, Archduke Franz Ferdinand, heir to the Austro-Hungarian throne and his wife Sophie, arrived by train in the Bosnian capital of Sarajevo. Franz Ferdinand was to inspect soldiers on summer manoeuvres nearby after which, accompanied by the mayor, he would drive through streets decorated with flags and flowers, acknowledging the crowds.

Some six years previously the empire of Austria-Hungary had formally annexed the provinces of Bosnia and Herzegovina, at the time under the control of the Ottoman Empire. This action had lead to much unrest and understandably the archduke's visit in 1914 was not appreciated by everyone, many considering Franz-Ferdinand and Sophie's presence an insult, particularly as their visit coincided with Serbian National Day. Hidden in the cheering crowds were seven young Bosnian Serbs, members of a terrorist organisation called the Black Hand, whose sole aim was the creation of a Greater Serbia. To bring attention to their cause they'd long planned to assassinate some well-known public figure, now the visit of the archduke and his wife provided them with the ideal opportunity.

As the cavalcade of six open-topped cars drove between cheering crowds, a bomb, thrown by 19-year old student Nedeljko Cabrinovic at the duke and duchess, missed its target. Swiftly, the Royal car accelerated way and the bomb exploded in the road injuring the following car's occupants and showering spectators with shrapnel. Shaken by the event, the archduke and his duchess nevertheless carried on to City Hall where the mayor nervously began his speech of welcome. Suddenly the archduke interrupted, shouting angrily: *'So this is how you welcome your guests – with bombs.'*

Speeches ended, Franz Ferdinand announced his wish to visit the hospital where the injured had been taken, insisting that the driver take an alternative route away from where the bombing had occurred. Unfortunately he and his wife were taken along the same route by which they'd arrived. The driver, on being ordered to turn back, stopped, directly in front of Gavrilo Princip, one of seven assassins planted around the town. Princip drew a gun and shot both Franz Ferdinand and Sophie who had vainly tried to protect her husband. Sophie died immediately and by 11am, Franz Ferdinand was bleeding to death from a bullet wound in the neck.

At his trial Gavrilo Princip stated: *'I am a Yugoslav nationalist, aiming for the unification of all Yugoslavs, and I do not care what form of state, but it must be freed from Austria.'* At 19 years old he was too young for the death sentence and instead was imprisoned for twenty years, eventually dying of tuberculosis in 1918.

This incident was the catalyst which led to the First World War. Within weeks Russia mobilised in support of the Serbs after Austria bombed Belgrade, Germany declared war on Russia in support of Austria-Hungary and France declared war on Germany. In order to reach France, Germany entered neutral Belgium, a country Britain had pledged to uphold under the Treaty of London of 1839, later referred to by German Chancellor Theobald von Bethmann-Hollweg as a mere 'scrap of paper'.

In London on 3 August 1914, Lord Edward Grey, Foreign Secretary, stood before the House of Commons detailing the situation which had accelerated with frightening speed in Europe. Returning to his Whitehall office he watched as gas lamps were lit below in the Mall commenting to his companion, *'the lamps are going out, all over Europe. We shall not see them lit again in our lifetime.'*

With Germany demanding passage through its borders Belgium, under the 1839 Treaty, immediately appealed for Britain's help. A prompt request that Germany recognize Belgium's impartiality was despatched. Receiving no response, the Government, prompted by fears for national security, had no alternative but to demand that Germany withdraw its forces or face the consequences. The request was ignored, the army marched on and just before midnight on the 4 August, Britain declared war on Germany.

Very quickly the Government extended the Bank Holiday by three days, with banks and the Stock Exchange closing to deal with ongoing demands from investors. Families returning home by train from their holidays were surprised to find themselves surrounded by regular soldiers and reservists on their way to their headquarters. To deal with what could have easily developed into chaos, the Government immediately introduced the Defence of the Realm Act (DORA) legislation which would have frequent additions during the war years.

Lord Kitchener whose impassioned call for men to sign up encouraged thousands to step forward.

On 7 August, Field Marshal Earl Kitchener, appointed Secretary of State for War by Prime Minister Herbert Asquith, appealed for 100,000 single men aged between the ages of nineteen and thirty to do their patriotic duty and join the Army. The British Army at that time had 710,000 men, including reserves, of which 80,000 were regular troops; it had quickly been recognised that more men were needed. By 28 August, a further appeal went out for another 100,000 men to join up. News of Kitchener's request spread rapidly and, buoyed up by a great wave of enthusiasm, street celebrations broke out with dense crowds of cheering men and women waving flags and singing patriotic songs. Why did these young men join up in their thousands? Was war seen as an adventure, a chance to win the admiration of their women, a chance for heroism, an opportunity, for some, to escape poverty and hunger? All around them friends they'd grown up were similarly eager to join the military ranks, no one wanting to appear cowardly.

Patriotism was a major factor, defending king, country and home was seen as a way of protecting all Great Britain stood for in 1914. King George V was much loved, known for his sense of duty and his love of home life and loyalty to these laudable values may have been uppermost in many volunteers' minds as they accepted the king's shilling.

There were some dissenters, however. A leaflet distributed by the Neutrality League read: *'Englishmen do your duty and keep your country out of a wicked and stupid war.'* Conscientious objectors would not fight on ethical or religious grounds, their belief in pacifism, or simply an inability to kill another human being. These shirkers or conchies as they later became known were the subject of hate campaigns, refused service in shops and public houses, verbally abused on the streets, or handed a white feather, a symbol of cowardice, by girls and women who'd actively seek out anyone who looked as though they should have joined the forces.

A 1914 King's shilling – when accepted it symbolised acceptance of a man's commitment to king and country.

Volunteer numbers increased substantially when a shocked public learnt that Britain and France had lost to the enemy at the Battle of Mons on 23 August 1914 with over 1,600 British soldiers dead,

Devastation comes to a Scarborough street in December 1914.

wounded or missing. It brought home to many who'd hesitated that there was a very real threat to their homes and loved ones. An event just before Christmas 1914 was another major factor in strengthening the forces. German battle cruisers had shelled Hartlepool, Scarborough and Whitby leaving 137 people dead and 592 injured. With these violent acts the war had well and truly arrived on the home front.

A national newspaper assured its readers that the British were not intimidated. *'The nation is not taken aback. The German belief that a show of force on the coast can demoralise the British people is a pitiful delusion,'* its report read.

German newspapers understandably took another view, praising its navy for a 'courageous attack' and 'proof of the gallantry of its navy'. The British press quickly denounced them as *'German ghouls, gloating over the murder of English schoolboys and the wanton war on women and children.'*

With full-page pictures of bombed houses and headlines exhorting MEN OF BRITAIN, WILL YOU STAND FOR THIS, and REMEMBER SCARBOROUGH!, recruitment offices experienced a further rush of volunteers with friends, neighbours and work colleagues signing up to what became known as the Pals regiments. By the end of 1915 over 2,466,719 men had volunteered and undergone training.

And what of those at home, women who before the war had mainly worked in domestic service, who when they married, were expected to give up work and remain at home as wives, mothers and housekeepers? None could have seen that by the end of the conflict approximately 1,600,000 women would undertake what had previously been looked upon as solely male occupations. The first women police officers and post women would be on the streets, women would operate buses and trams, drive vans, work on the railways as porters or maintenance crew, serve in shops, act as office clerks, or risk their lives in the highly dangerous surroundings of munitions factories where at least 950,000 women would go on to produce eighty per cent of the armaments the UK required. Equally important was the indispensable role women played in agriculture helping to keep the country in food.

Over 90,000 women volunteered for the Red Cross and many Voluntary Aid Detachments (VADS) trained in first aid and nursing, would cross the seas where they witnessed the frightful effects of war. Others drove ambulances, worked as welfare officers, nursed in auxiliary hospitals and convalescent homes, or assisted in providing meals and assistance for the wounded arriving home at railway stations.

Men, considered either too young or too old or working in reserved occupations, such as the clergy, coalmines, munitions factories and shipyards, would also see major changes with some occupations considered of national importance and exempt from call up at the start of the war, though less so as the need for men increased. Even men once considered medically unfit would, towards the end of the war, be accepted.

By December 1914, it was obvious that the war that should have been over by Christmas – a belief incidentally, supported by both sides – was not going to end as thought. No one could have imagined as 1915 arrived that another four years would pass before peace finally came.

It would be to a very different world that the men would return, a post-war world that would shake to the very foundations the rigid class system which had existed for centuries and one where the roles of women and men would draw closer together than ever before.

CHAPTER 3

1914
The Effect at Home

With the declaration of war on 4 August 1914 newspapers in Britain were quick to react carrying advertisements appealing to all men loyal to their homeland to sign up. Posters appeared 'There's Room for You, Fall in and Enlist Today', and 'Women of Britain say Go', to name just two. To further encourage enlistment, young men were told they would be serving alongside friends, an idea first suggested by General Sir Henry Rawlinson who was to play a major role in the Battle of the Somme and the Battle of Amiens. Pals Battalions proved a popular idea, leading to thousands joining up together, the outcome being that some villages would, in years to come, lose all their young men to the war.

The issue now was where they would train; as well as existing training grounds new facilities were urgently needed. Within a very short time land and property was requisitioned and camps built. In the meantime, recruits were housed in tents, billeted in towns or private homes but with winter fast approaching this situation had to change and change quickly.

A soldier reacting to the sudden and shocking bombings of Scarborough, Hartlepool and Whitby on 16 December felt the need to put the event into a poem, no doubt shaming even more who had hesitated into signing up.

> *'So we must keep plugging away,*
> *Yet all the while we practise the smile*
> *That will welcome the dawn of 'The Day'*
> *So many brave lives go under,*
> *But all know the job must be done –*
> *The debt will be paid for the Scarborough raid,*
> *By the men behind the gun.'*

And with the German army laying waste to Belgian cities and horrifying accounts of its people being murdered on the streets appearing in the press, as the year drew to a close Britain was welcoming thousands of refugees fleeing the atrocities. The War Refugees Committee (WRC), on appealing for accommodation, received 100,000 offers in just two weeks with every city, town and village ready to take in its share of refugee families.

Oswestry in 1914

It wasn't long before the people of Oswestry saw the first of many changes they would experience in the coming months and years. The rumour that Park Hall and its extensive acres a short distance from the town had been handed over for use as a training base by its owner was confirmed as correct. Word had it that shortly 14,000 men were due to arrive; within weeks that number upped to 21,000 men, plus 400 to 500 officers.

The *Oswestry and Border Counties Advertizer* was quick to announce on 5 August that henceforth it would publish news from both home and abroad in special editions, as well as posting notices on their Caxton Press premises and at the Cross, a conjunction of streets in the centre of town. Movement of troops however, would not be made public, in line with Government restrictions.

With men leaving for wartime service, local businesses were anxious to assure customers that it was business as usual and help would be given to the cause. Messrs H. Jones & Son, Oil Dealers, Middleton Road, assured customers that the business would carry on despite the fact three partners in the firm had been called upon to serve, whilst a dentist, aware of restrictions on recruits joining up if they had bad teeth, was offering to provide *'Teeth to the amount of £100 free of all charges available to all intending recruits who were unable to enlist through defective teeth providing that they produced an Army Medical Officer's Certificate and would enlist and be accepted afterwards.'*

Comforts for soldiers was the subject of a meeting held in the Guildhall, presided over by Mrs Williams, the mayoress, and Lady Harlech. *'Her Majesty the Queen,'* the mayoress told the packed audience, *'has requested that ladies countrywide make and repair garments for soldiers, sailors, Territorials and the wounded.'* Lady Harlech then detailed what clothing was needed commenting that *'she was sure, seeing the large numbers present, that it was the wish of every lady in Oswestry and district to comply with Her Majesty's wish and do all they possibly could to relieve the needs of the soldiers in the provision of clothing.'*

This need for comforts was addressed by local children later in the year with a large consignment of knitted woollen cuffs, mufflers and socks they had made sent to the British Red Cross Society from where they would be forwarded to sailors serving with the North Sea Fleet. The enthusiasm with which women answered the call for knitted items was not always looked upon with favour however, one soldier felt moved to write that *'some of the items are vastly uncomfortable, lumpy and itchy'.*

The Guildhall, Oswestry today. Hundreds gathered in front of it to hear news of the war. (Bob Johnstone)

On 19 August a police statement relating to aliens in the town appeared in the *Advertizer*'s public notices.

'Specific to the area, German subjects who are not naturalised are required to register at the nearest police station. House owners are also required to notify the police of any German subject staying in their household and are warned against harbouring any such, owners of motor garages are prohibited from hiring or lending cars to any German subject. Finally the public are requested to immediately inform the police of any suspicious alien who may be resident or passing through the county.'

Understandably, this notice caused much consternation; any foreigner living locally was now watched with suspicion even if previously they had been a friend. In the early days of the war, so hated was the word 'German' that even German measles became known as the Belgium Flush.

In September 1914 the *Advertizer* under the headline OSWESTRY 'PALS' RECRUITING CAMPAIGN announced that a meeting would be held at the Cross for the furtherance of the Pals movement. It was hoped eligible young men such as clerks and shop assistants would sign up with local recruiter Colour Sergeant E.J. Evans. Made clear was the fact that *'in all probability, volunteers would be soldiered together, drilled together, instructed together and trained together.'*

Thursday, 3 September saw the official departure of the regular troops of the Shropshire Imperial Yeomanry seen off by Mr W.H. Spaull, deputy mayor, other dignitaries and townspeople. It was noted that *'officers and men were cheery and optimistic in spirit and their merry humour dried many a tear-filled eye of relatives and friends taking their farewells.'*

The Oswestry Pals' appeal at the beginning of September had been highly successful, on the afternoon of Monday, 7 September 162 young men paraded in front of enthusiastic crowds in Cae Glas Park. They sang songs, a favourite being 'It's a long way to Tipperary', before Colour Sergeant Evans drew them to attention in fours to hear the deputy mayor and Lord Harlech address them. Speeches ended the men marched smartly out of Cae Glas Park led by the town band and made their way through cheering crowds to the railway station, within

The Cross, Oswestry, scene of recruitment meetings for the Pals.

Cae Glas Park, Oswestry before the war. The entrance gates became a memorial to the fallen at the end of the war.

minutes of arriving they had boarded a train and were awaiting its departure.

As it drew out of the station, men hung out of the carriage windows waving frantically, anxious to stay within sight of their loved ones to the very last minute. One volunteer, having paused to get a drink of water was nearly left behind having to leap onto the footplate as the train drew away. The last crowds on the platform saw of the train carrying away their men was a large Union Jack covering the rear carriage. How many of those bidding goodbye on that day must have comforted each other with the phrase 'well, it'll all be over by Christmas'.

By September Oswestry Cottage Hospital's facilities were feeling the strain of coping with military personnel as well as civilians. Thirteen Territorials had needed treatment within the month, and for a hospital highly dependent on money funded by an annual ball, cancelled in 1914, and carnivals, it meant alternative ways of raising money were needed to keep going. Fortunately an urgent appeal resulted in enough money raised to solve the current problem.

In October 1914 rumours that a meeting to protest against residents of German origin being allowed to remain in Oswestry were circulating. By 7.30pm on a cold autumn night over 1,000 people assembled on Bailey Head near to the Guildhall but no speaker turned up. A workman however, made good progress collecting for the local war fund whilst a procession of little boys waving flags caused amusement as they preceded the dispersing crowd through the streets.

In autumn Oswestry was preparing to receive its first Belgium refugees with ladies organised to take care of the families as they arrived. Two houses were made ready in Duke Street, an area housing mostly railway workers. An appeal for donations returned a good result with townsfolk, appalled by newspaper accounts of the atrocities the families had suffered, *'glad to show their help in the usual fashion'*. The first refugees arrived by train at the beginning of October and were taken in a wagonette to their new home accompanied by welcoming cheers from a large crowd. The party included two men, two women and eight children, the latter said to be *'happy and smiling and in possession of many toys'*.

With news that shortly 1,000 men would be arriving, all of whom would need short-term accommodation, public buildings in the town were swiftly requisitioned. Several Sunday schools together with the Memorial Hall would be utilised to house battalions of soldiers, whilst the Assembly Rooms and Christ Church were put at the disposal of the Territorials for rest, reading, writing and amusements. Three buildings within the town were also earmarked for use as military hospitals in the event of an invasion.

The art school in Arthur Street was taken over with volunteers brought in to produce clothing for the military under the patronage of Lady Harlech. Here, in just one week, 244 garments were cut out and a further 101 sent out to be made up at home.

The need to entertain the large number of troops about to be billeted in the town was quickly recognised resulting in the formation of a Social Service League. Musical programmes were organised with the local band performing both popular and patriotic music regularly in Cae Glas Park bandstand. Before long military musicians were returning the compliment quipping that the entertained had become for once, the entertainers. Music was a popular way to draw in crowds and raise money with a summer concert for the Red Cross in the Victoria Assembly Rooms well-attended by dignitaries and townspeople and

The Memorial Hall, Oswestry opened in 1906, as it is today. (Bob Johnstone)

Christ Church, Oswestry put at the disposal of the Territorials during the First World War.

proceeds amounting to £12 15s 6d. In his speech the mayor said it made him feel that Oswestry was not behind in support of the Red Cross.

In October local MP W.C. Bridgman, visiting families whose men had left for the front, was shocked to see the hardships they were experiencing. Some of the women he met were not aware they were entitled to claim a separation allowance made available from Government, with some admitting they didn't know how to make an application, others not liking to ask for fear of being turned down. Discovering that funding in the area had been held up, sometimes for five weeks or more, Mr Bridgman asked that regular visits be made to every family *'there are many willing workers only waiting to be told how they can be used,'* he commented, *'and here at any rate, is one outlet for their energy.'*

As December drew nearer realisation that their men would not be home for Christmas was recognised and families were seeking gifts to send to soldiers and sailors abroad. Oswestry shops Hobleys and Dales Brothers Emporium, were advertising suitable items advising that anything purchased from them would be sent free of charge under the *Advertizer*'s postage scheme which had undertaken to ensure all items reached their destination.

A letter to an Oswestry mother from her son in the trenches at the end of the year described the circumstances in which the Tommies found themselves.

> *'They are giving us a bit of a rest now. We have been in the thick of the fight ever since we came here. Now we have got half a company in the trenches, the other half in reserve about 100 yards behind. While I am writing this my pal and myself are waiting for the old "canteen" to boil. We are boiling a piece of fat bacon, so as not to cause a smoke. I can assure you it is a luxury to have a drop of tea.*
>
> *Jack Johnsons* [heavy German artillery shells named after a US heavyweight boxing champion] *are dropping all around us. They make a hole big enough to bury six to ten men. Every farm is burnt to the ground by the Germans, I wish I could tell you where we are, but you see I dare not. Never mind, I will tell you all when I come home – if I have the luck.'*

Let's hope he did.

Whitchurch in 1914
On 8 August two notices appeared in the *Whitchurch Herald*, one announced the cancellation of a Flower Show on 12 August in Ash, a village south of town *'owing to the War, until further notice'*. The other, placed by the Soldiers' and Sailors' Families Association, requested that the names of all soldiers, sailors and reservists who had been called up be supplied as soon as possible to the association secretary. Already changes, which would only increase as the months passed, were impacting on the lives of people in both town and borough.

Before long the local Yeomanry and Territorials left Whitchurch for garrison duty in various locations and rumours that the Cheshire Brigade of the Royal Field Artillery, some 400 strong, would be billeted in the town over the weekend were causing great excitement. Arriving in atrocious wet weather the men were housed in the Town Hall and public houses around the town; the fifty cannon brought with them were stored in the Smithfield. The following day, watched by cheering crowds, the brigade moved on, thanking the townsfolk for the hospitality they had received.

Since the call for men had gone out Whitchurch recruitment had progressed steadily with a good response to the initial call to arms. Lieutenant J.H. Smith, a former sergeant instructor, reported that the men were quite cheerful and happy and a donation of cigarettes sent to them by Mr Wilson of Green End had been greatly appreciated.

A recruitment meeting held in August in Egerton Drill Hall, specifically aimed at the young men of Whitchurch, attracted a large and enthusiastic audience who listened intently as Major Godsal from Wrexham gave details of the army Lord Kitchener was raising. Local cheese factor Mr E.P. Norton offered his cheese warehouse for drilling purposes and by the end of the evening over a hundred men had signed up.

With prices of raw materials, together with availability, affecting industries, by September W.H. Smith and Company, an influential firm in Whitchurch, announced that price lists for their hardware had been withdrawn due to the fact they could no longer guarantee the prices shown. They did, however, reassure their customers that for as long as possible stock purchased prior to the war would be supplied at the old charges.

Collections for a variety of causes were by now regularly taking

Egerton Drill Hall, New Street, Whitchurch, now demolished. (courtesy of Peter Lea)

place in the town. A smoking concert held in September at the Fox and Goose Assembly Rooms, together with the Sunday collection at the Baptist Church, raised £1,120 in aid of the Prince of Wales National Relief Fund. It was considered that if every town in the country did as well as Whitchurch the grand total of the Fund would reach £8,000,000.

A letter published in the *Herald* proposing that ladies do a bit of recruiting themselves appeared in October. The writer advises:

> *'Make sure there are no "slackers", no "royal stand backs" and no "ready when they fetch me boys".'*
>
> *Take my tip girls, don't be seen in the company of a young man who is too chicken-hearted to don the King's uniform and do his "little bit" for the country. It is possible the Government in the very near future will bring pressure on the laggards. Don't let your sweetheart be amongst that lot, do the "gentle pressure business yourselves".'*

Mrs Pearce, organiser of the Alexandra Sewing Club who'd sent off a parcel of new clothing to Belgium, received a thank you letter in September from HRH the Duchess of Vendome, sister of King Albert I of Belgium. At the same time an appeal held in the town for the Belgian Relief Fund had resulted in £251 14s 11d this being sent to the Central Fund, WRC in London. Later collections were kept in the town to help with the imminent intake of refugees.

By mid-October news that the first Belgian refugees would shortly be arriving in the town led to a house quickly acquired, cleaned and furnished to receive them, a coal merchant promising to donate two hundredweight of coal and bakers, a loaf of bread per person per day for the duration of the family's stay. Broughall Cottage, which had also been placed at the disposal of Belgian refugees by owner Mr Storey, was however withdrawn due to 'the inability to find suitable persons'. In 1915 it would be opened as an auxiliary hospital.

By the end of the month Monsieur and Madam Gaston Ghys and Monsieur de Rear, together with their children had arrived. Originating from Ghent, they had been florists and seeds men until forced to flee their homes as the Germans advanced.

As with other towns and cities, in Whitchurch the Aliens Restriction Act was having an effect. Joseph Fulgoni, an Italian who had lived in Whitchurch for ten years found himself the subject of false rumours concerning his opinions on the war. Anxious to put the record straight, he had published in the *Herald* a public notice offering a £5 reward to anyone who could help him trace the instigator of the stories concerning him and his family, at the same time reminding readers that Italy had declared itself neutral.

Pupils at the Whitchurch Girls' High School arrived one morning to find part of their games field ploughed up in order to grow potatoes. A motto hung in the cookery room also used as a dining room instructed the girls to 'Laugh and grow fat, and eat less', a reminder that food shortages were already a problem and there was an urgent need for frugality in their eating habits. Extra lessons quickly added to the pupils' curriculum covered first aid, bandaging and poultry keeping whilst they were allowed to knit socks and mittens for soldiers when awaiting their turn in the end of term music examinations. The school took in two Belgian refugee pupils, Miss Lauwers and Miss Guys –

difficult for them no doubt as they spoke no English and their fellow schoolgirls no Flemish.

November, and a Lantern Lecture written by F.G. Mackenzie, war correspondent of the *Daily Mail* attracted a large audience. A report the following week stated *'despite broken slides and a cracked lens in the lantern, the spectators were said to have enjoyed the slides made from photographs taken on the battlefield'*. What they saw must have shocked many of the spectators, bringing home to them the dangers their loved ones were facing.

The *Herald* informed its readers in autumn that a copy of their newspaper had arrived in trenches occupied by the 1st Battalion of the KSLI where it was reportedly 'scrambled' for eagerly. Asked by a sergeant if there were any Whitchurch men in the trench everyone answered yes, anxious to get their hands on home news.

A member of the British Expeditionary Force (BEF) hailing from Whitchurch sent a letter to the *Herald* with a harrowing account of the conditions he and his friends were experiencing. Home must have been on his mind, *'I can't imagine what Whitchurch is like with hardly anyone on the streets as so many of us are at the front,'* he writes, ending by saying, *'I wonder if we'll be home by Christmas, don't know if I'll manage it but there seems to be every prospect from the present position. German prisoners are coming in to where I am stationed, boys of about fifteen years old.'*

In November at Whitchurch Dairy Association Annual Show over 2,000 cheeses entered from both Shropshire and Cheshire were judged. No doubt with the conflict uppermost in the judges' minds a flavoursome Cheshire was described as having a 'real military aroma' which would 'provoke the highest admiration of Mr Thomas Atkins'.

With the industry currently doing well, a gift of one ton of cheese was made to the Army. Valued at £100, it was shipped over to France with a promise of more to come nearer to Christmas. One man commented that at least half the amount should go to the Navy who were doing an equally important job guarding the coasts and maintaining the country's food supplies.

By the end of November the question of reduced drinking hours brought in under DORA in August was being discussed at the Petty Sessions. The bench's considered opinion was that due to Whitchurch's record of sobriety there was no need for action. A request was made however, that extra liquor should not be provided to women and soldiers, with local police asked to keep a check on the latter.

The first firm confirmation of an encampment on Prees Heath was made in the press at the end of November 1914, although initially it was not known if it was for British troops or German prisoners. It wasn't long before local people learnt that there would indeed be a training camp erected for Lord Kitchener's army. The area was considered particularly appropriate with a main road and railway adjacent to the site.

At the beginning of December Sir Wyndham Hanmer of the Army Remount Service, addressing a meeting of farmers at Whitchurch Cheese Show, told the gathering that he was most concerned that some families did not realise the great need for recruits or the danger Britain was facing. *'There are able-bodied young fellows who have done nothing towards assisting to keep the enemy from these shores,'* he told his audience, *'and their farms would not be worth a snap of the fingers to them if the Germans got a foothold in this country.'*

Not long afterwards, a well-attended meeting in the Egerton Drill Hall chaired by Mr C.T. Dugdale of nearby Terrick Hall, with various military personnel present, proved that a great many young men from Whitchurch and the neighbourhood were anxious to know how best to be of some use to their country. Explaining that the King had called for 100,000 men to form a second army, Mr Dugdale told them it was therefore their first duty to readily enlist especially as for the moment recruitment for the Yeomanry and Territorials had been stopped. Later, it was reported in the *Shrewsbury Chronicle* that Whitchurch had made a splendid response to the call to arms with *'many of her gallant sons giving proof of their pluck and determination that will eventually result in crushing Prussian militarism.'* Sir Wyndham Hanmer's message must have hit home.

A message sent from a soldier in the 5th (Service) Battalion KSLI in December gave news of Whitchurch Pals currently billeted in the village of Chiddingfold, Surrey near to training grounds. He writes:

'The Whitchurch men are practically all together and doing well except that some of them are still suffering to some extent from the effects of vaccination and inoculation. At first we had to draw rations from the "Cook House", a bit of a tent some distance

away and it was a game dishing the food out. Conditions are changed now for the better, we are engaged in field work, making the best use of ground when attacking or advancing and it is very interesting though somewhat arduous running across ploughed fields.'

The wife of a major was up before the Petty Sessions late December 1914 charged with driving a motor car along the Prees Heath road, now part of the A41, at the excessive speed of thirty-five miles per hour. She denied the car could reach such speeds, her husband backing her by saying as it had been snowing he'd warned her to drive slowly. Nevertheless, she was fined £2.

Although many were probably not in a festive mood, with Christmas not far away local shopkeepers were advertising gifts and cards reminding buyers that they needed to post them promptly if they were to reach their destination overseas in time for Christmas Day. Seasonal markets were also taking place on 18 December albeit with a greatly reduced selection of produce for sale.

Towards the end of December a notice of two meetings headed 'Women and the War – How can they help?' was held at Church House by the League of Honour. Five months into the war and already there was a need for women to step away from traditional roles and take over occupations once considered only suitable for men, a need which would increase a thousand-fold in the years to come.

And at the front, on Christmas Day 1914 British and German soldiers called an unofficial ceasefire. Across no man's land the Tommies could see German trenches lined with decorated trees and soon they were joining in with their enemies, singing carols and meeting in no man's land to exchange gifts, chocolate, tinned goods, cigars and cigarettes; even a makeshift football match took place. Two days later, the participants were once again shooting each other.

An embossed brass box containing an enclosed card reading 'With best wishes for a victorious New Year from Princess Mary and friends at home' together with gifts such as cigarettes, tobacco or chocolates, was sent out to everyone wearing the King's uniform at the end of the year. Also entitled to the gift were wounded men in hospital or on leave, prisoners of war were presented with the box when they returned home.

In all two and a half million embossed brass boxes were distributed,

1914 THE EFFECT AT HOME 45

the money raised by an appeal carried out by 17-year-old Princess Mary for the Sailors and Soldiers Christmas Fund.

In Britain, the strain of the first year of the conflict was beginning to have an effect with new rules and regulations to absorb and menfolk in the forces to worry about. It was not surprising some could not deal with the situation and took to drink, when they could get it, to help them cope. Drunkenness was a big issue during the war years; understandably it would only increase as the conflict continued.

Brass box and card, a gift instigated by Princess Mary.

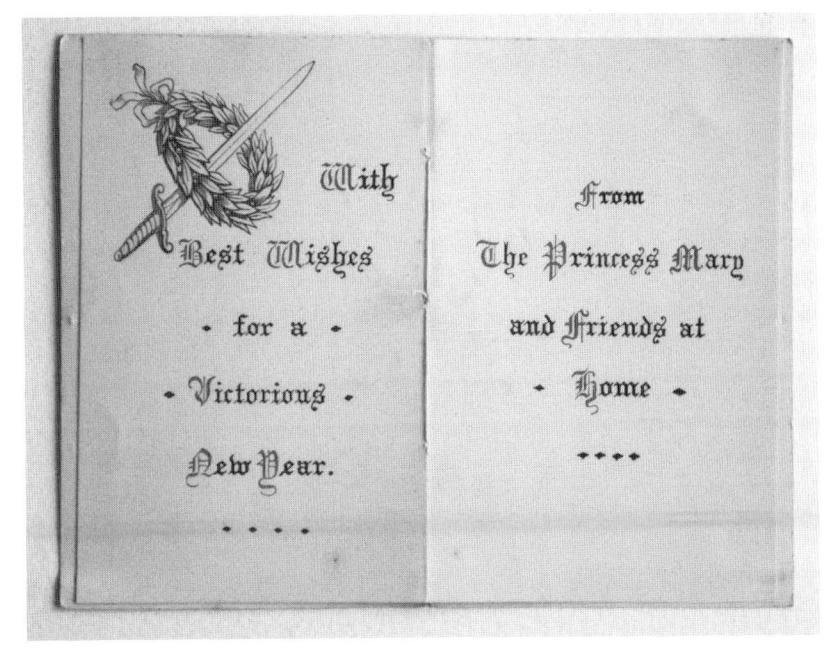

Four years would pass with many thousands sacrificed on all sides before peace was finally declared and men were able to return, if they could, to a normal family life. By then working class men who had fought shoulder to shoulder with their 'betters' in the trenches had realised that they had an equal right to be heard, and did not want to return to the servile roles they had occupied before the war. Women too had experienced a new freedom working in factories or on the land and had realised there were better options available to them. The strict class system which had kept a large part of society in a deferential role pre-war was beginning to crumble and it was destined never to return.

CHAPTER 4

Shropshire's Main Military Camps

Park Hall Camp, Oswestry
Built in the 1560s, Park Hall, near Oswestry must have been an impressive sight in its heyday. The first thing seen on entering the hall would have been dark oak panelled walls, a canopied fireplace and a twenty-foot table under which were kept crossbows, a cannon and mantraps.

Park Hall, Oswestry. Built in 1560, in 1914 it was handed over by its owner for war use.

With the outbreak of war Major Wynne Corrie, the owner of Park Hall who had been trying to sell it, promptly took it off the market and handed it over to the War Office. The first Oswestry residents heard of the hall's change of use was via a report in the local paper in November 1914. Very shortly, it announced, 14,000 troops would be billeted at the hall; within two weeks reports had upped the number of men expected to 21,000 troops and 500 officers.

Building work began promptly, despite a particularly wet and wretched winter, with over 900 labourers employed from both the local area and further afield. Within weeks the grounds surrounding the hall were transformed with roads and hutments and a water supply. Included in the works was a railway loop line undertaken by the Cambrian Railways Company, the military taking over to build the final portion into the camp.

By the beginning of 1915 the construction of Park Hall Military Camp was progressing well with the builders, Messrs Wilson, Lovatt and Sons advertising for more labour, *'Wanted, good Builder's Labourers, wages 6d per hour.'* Before long the company was inundated with men presenting themselves on site for this guaranteed work.

It was planned that by the time building was completed the camp would contain not only numerous huts to house the men, but also,

Hutments at Park Hall Camp, Oswestry.

The road through Park Hall Camp, Oswestry leading to the hospital.

served by a wide road, a military hospital with 866 beds, photographers' studios, cinemas and shops. YMCA huts dedicated to serving the troops would also be constructed together with a well-appointed theatre to entertain the soldiers, the first in the country, incidentally, to receive the name Garrison Theatre.

By July 1915 4,000 troops from the Royal Welsh Fusiliers and the Cheshire Regiment were disembarking from trains at a station some three miles away in Whittington, famous for its castle. It was reported that they marched from the station with the Fusiliers' mascot, a goat, leading the way.

The men were housed in the first huts to be completed in the grounds whilst their officers took over the hall as their mess. From then on, Park Hall Camp went on to train thousands of troops prior to their being sent to the front line.

The Scottish Regimental Band welcomed in the New Year 1916 in the traditional way with men assembling on the camp parade ground to hear a variety of Scottish airs. As twelve o'clock struck Auld Lang Syne was sung before 'lights out' was called and the men returned to their billets.

Picturesque ruins of Whittingham Castle near Oswestry. Men arriving at the railway station would have seen these as they marched from the railway station to Park Hall Camp.

By now the camp was very much part of life in Oswestry and the surrounding areas although there were health concerns as can be seen from a letter which appeared in the local paper. Headed WHAT IS WRONG AT OSWESTRY, the writer questions the unsatisfactory death rate of nearly sixty men at the camp within two months.

> *'Let us remember, this is a case of the death of picked men, mostly, we believe, under the age of twenty-one years. They came from farmers' homes, from schools and colleges, and all before joining the Camp, were regarded as "Class A". Yet, in less than a month after joining they have been carried back home to be buried.*
>
> *Is the Camp sanitation bad? Are the huts (if any) unfit for habitation? Or, if in billets, are these badly selected, are the men crowded together in excess of what is regarded as the minimum space requisite for healthy habitation? Are the local health authorities aware of the alarming death rate? If so, have any steps been taken to see what is wrong?*
>
> *Our people are ready to accept the fortunes of war, but in the course of preparation for services, some guarantee should be given against the slaughter of their boys at home. What has the War Office to say?'*

It wasn't until the following year that the Under Secretary of State for War was asked to make enquiries into the conditions of soldiers stationed at the camp. It resulted in a report which identified causes of death as mainly due to pulmonary conditions brought about by the close proximity of the men, the wet and cold environment and bad ventilation.

Meanwhile at Park Hall, entertainment for the soldiers in YMCA hut two had been greatly enhanced by the presentation of a gramophone and records from Dr Withers of nearby Chirk. *'If the donor could have seen the group of men collected around the 'phone on Sunday afternoon,'* read a letter to the press from the camp, *'he would realise that such a gift is not likely to lack appreciation.'*

By the end of 1916 the camp was well established with men passing through it regularly on their way to the front. Entertainers attended every week to give concerts and as the end of the year approached,

YMCA huts and staff at Park Hall Camp, Oswestry.

A hut lavishly decorated for Christmas at Park Hall Camp, Oswestry.

with Christmas not far away, the men took the opportunity to decorate their huts with swathes of garlands hanging from the ceiling, crackers on the table and suitable messages such as 'Good Luck to our Navy' and 'Success to the Loyals at the Front' displayed for all to see.

By 1917 a routine was established in Park Hall Camp with new men arriving on a regular basis for training whilst others moved on to the front.

A report that some of the men belonging to a Lancashire battalion were either stone deaf, one-eyed or short-legged was causing concern however. *'More and more men are being taken on at Park Hall without the question being asked wouldn't they be of better use to the country if they were employed in civilian occupations,'* stated one report. An answer from the War Office eventually arrived: *'We have received no complaints and any such men unfit for military service would be discharged from the Army forthwith,'* it responded curtly.

In 1918 the end of Park Hall came suddenly and unexpectedly. On the evening of Boxing Day 1918 a fierce fire broke out located in a wooden beam in a small chapel housed in the main building. It was later thought that an electrical wiring fault had ignited the tinder-dry wood. The fire spread rapidly along the wooden frontage of the building, with both Oswestry and Shrewsbury fire appliances attending as rapidly as they could. Due to the lack of water available, the old building was virtually destroyed, although a later Victorian extension to the hall still stood the following day despite being beyond repair. The Army was exonerated of any blame for the fire, although its loss did lead to wild rumours with some locals saying that German prisoners may have set the buildings alight.

At the beginning of 1919 Park Hall was in use as a prisoner of war camp. There had been a lot of unrest at the camp since the peace had been signed, with German prisoners, encouraged by their officers, refusing to attend roll call and generally behaving in an unruly fashion. On the morning of Saturday, 14 July 1919 no prisoners had paraded for roll call leading to reinforcements from the Royal Defence Corps being called in to help sentries on the site.

A German prisoner of war, 20-year-old Willie Oster, together with several hundred other prisoners, began throwing stones and bricks at Private Maycock, the lone sentry on duty. Fearing a riot and first warning the prisoners to stop, he fired his rifle into the air to summon

The Royal Defence Corps provided security and undertook guard duties in Britain during the conflict. Note the hut under construction in the background.

help. The unrest continued and Private Maycock again fired into the air aiming for the roof of a latrine, totally unaware that Willie Oster had climbed onto the roof. Oster died from the bullet which passed through two sheets of iron and two boards before entering his head, killing him instantly.

At an inquest, the jury returned a verdict of death by misadventure and exonerated Private Maycock from any blame. Willie Oster was buried with full military honours in a small prisoner of war cemetery in the grounds of Park Hall and in later years his remains were moved to the Cannock Chase German War Cemetery in Staffordshire.

Life at the camp before the last prisoner left for home in November 1919 did have its better moments, for amongst the 6,000 prisoners housed there one recorded in his diary that despite access to the privy being through ankle deep mud, frozen water to wash in and badly made cocoa, prisoners were not that badly treated. Many of them worked on local farms or in forestry, whilst officers were allowed to organise a choir, play sports and arrange other entertainments. English newspapers were allowed, as was alcohol – not quite all the comforts of home but not that hard to endure.

The camp was in use as a demobilisation camp at the end of the war whilst the ruins of the burnt-out hall were left to fall into disrepair. The surrounding huts were removed with the exception of the camp hospital, these buildings eventually becoming part of the Shropshire Orthopaedic, now known as the Robert Jones and Agnes Hunt Hospital which is renowned throughout the world today for its pioneering work.

Just twenty years later with the outbreak of the Second World War, Park Hall was once again seeing huts being constructed and the military

Willie Oster's final resting place in Cannock Chase German Military Cemetery. (Bob Johnstone)

in control. It continued to be used until the Royal Artillery left in 1968 leaving the Infantry Junior Leaders in occupation until it was eventually closed in December 1975.

Prees Heath Camp
News that a training camp for 14,000 men was to be constructed on Prees Heath Common first reached the ears of Whitchurch residents in late November 1914. The common was in an ideal situation, dry and sandy with a good water supply, close to a main road with a railway in the vicinity and not far from the town of Whitchurch. Initially there was some doubt as to whether it would be for British troops or German prisoners but its use was confirmed as a training camp by December 1914. Construction began, with between 200 and 300 men constructing small rails and erecting wooden huts.

With huts going up with all speed news was out that three brigades of infantry numbering up to 12,000 men, a number approximately three times the population of nearby Whitchurch, from the Engineers, Army Service Corps and possibly the Cavalry would be taking up residence early 1915.

As Christmas approached a plea went out from the War Office requesting that all artisans and other workers building the Prees Heath hutments continue to work through the Christmas holidays with just a few hours of relaxation on Christmas Day. *'It is of the utmost importance to find shelter at the earliest possible date for those who are serving their country in this hour of peril, those of us who make some sacrifice of leisure or comfort are but contributing in a much smaller degree to those who have volunteered for service in the field in the defence of the country,'* read a report in the press.

By the second week January 1915, over 150 huts, situated either side of the Chester to Shrewsbury main road, were virtually complete except for windows and the ruberoid roofing. The camp would eventually house 900 huts, over sixty feet long and twenty feet wide, each capable of housing thirty men. A large workforce was taken on from all over the country, many lodging in Whitchurch, transported daily by wagons to the site with joiners earning 9½d an hour and labourers 7d.

By mid February hundreds of huts were lining the Shrewsbury to Chester road and the sandy common, formerly home to a variety of

Men in the course of constructing Prees Heath Camp, Whitchurch. (courtesy of Peter Lea)

Staff working in the pharmacy attached to the hospital at Prees Heath Camp, Whitchurch. (courtesy of Peter Lea)

wildlife and brushwood, was transformed. Over a thousand men were now involved in building, not only huts, but also stables, shops, photographers, a cinema, and a brick-built hospital consisting of nine main wings with pharmacy and operating theatre. Water and sewerage facilities were installed and roads laid to allow efficient movement around the area. The camp had its own electricity supply, something incidentally that Whitchurch did not receive until the 1930s.

Work had also started on a one-mile single-track branch line linking the London and North Western Railway (LNWR) Crewe and Shrewsbury line with a siding adjacent to the camp. This was much appreciated by the operators of Whitchurch Station Goods Yard which until then had been taking the strain of receiving huge amounts of materials intended for the camp before it was transported along increasingly deteriorating roads.

The first troops to occupy the huts arrived at Whitchurch station at the beginning of May with 200 men of the 11th Battalion, the Border Regiment (the Lonsdale Pals) sent from Carlisle. Together with their officers they marched the distance of some three miles to the camp cheered on by crowds lining the road. A further detachment, this time from the Highland Light Infantry arrived later in the week. By mid May Whitchurch was growing used to the sight of troops on its streets with local hostelries happy to invite them in. Already the town had formed an entertainments committee and at the camp the first YMCA huts had been opened and equipped for the comfort of the troops.

With the arrival of large numbers of men at Prees Heath Camp, cinemas had quickly been constructed for their entertainment. The Heath Cinema mid-year was showing a melodrama entitled 'Her Escape' to be followed by Charlie Chaplin's 'Knock-out', described as a *'screaming comedy in two parts'* whilst the Palace was presenting 'How Jack Johnson (boxer) Lost the Championship' followed by the 'Bugler Boy of Lancashire'.

By the end of August Prees Heath Camp was nearing completion with troops regularly arriving and by the end of the year it was anticipated that over 20,000 would be in residence.

In October the camp held a well-attended boxing tournament with Bombardier Billy Wells, British and British Empire Champion and the

Soldiers gather for a night out at the Palace Cinema, specially built at Prees Heath, Whitchurch. (courtesy of Peter Lea)

first heavyweight to win the Lonsdale Belt taking part. A report at the time confirmed that his opponent dodged around the ring with great agility but it was evident Wells was bent on doing no damage to his challenger.

But in December, the *Herald* was reporting that the camp was a *'veritable quagmire during the week on account of very heavy rains, locomotion by any means (other than boat which we understand has not yet been tried) is extremely difficult!'*

Christmas 1916 at the camp had been a quiet affair mainly due to the terrible weather in December. All the YMCA huts had been kept busy with the men making the best of the situation decorating their huts and making sure all enjoyed their day. Christmas and New Year services too, which took place in hut number four, bought for the camp by the people of Whitchurch, were well attended.

In March, a post office was constructed for the men greatly relieving pressure on the one in Whitchurch which had regularly received crowds of soldiers sending letters home. The camp post office reportedly sent out around 7,000 letters and postcards each week.

Bombardier Billy Wells, British and British Empire Heavyweight Champion, took part in boxing contests put on at Prees Heath Camp, Whitchurch. (Churchman's Cigarette Card)

By May, in line with similar problems at Park Hall, there were concerns about the number of deaths, thirty-eight, at the camp since the beginning of the year. The reason given was unhealthy conditions, but on official inspection, the camp was found to be suitable and adequate and the complaints were taken no further.

On a more cheerful note June saw a khaki wedding taking place in St Alkmund's Church, Whitchurch between Miss Owen from the Swan Hotel in the town and Private Wilson, currently stationed at the camp. The integration of camp personnel with the local population was now well and truly accepted.

In July a column in the *Herald* was praising soldiers for creating small gardens around their huts. The paper suggests, *'If the opportunity*

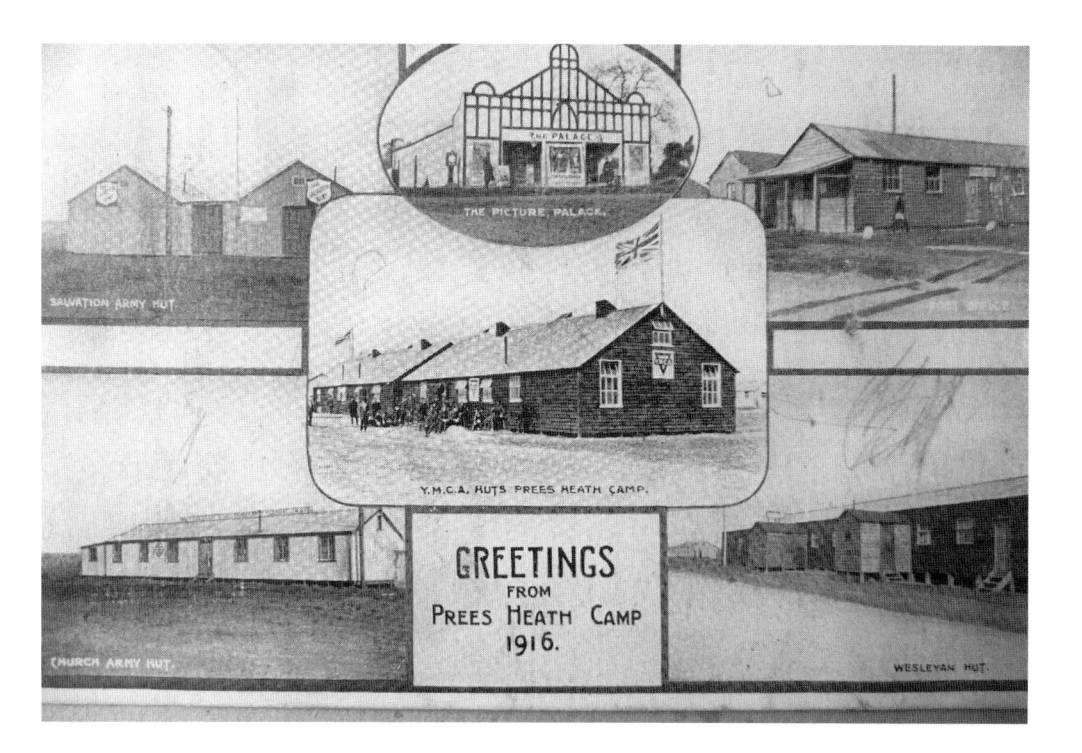

Two cards despatched from Prees Heath Camp post office. (courtesy of Peter Lea)

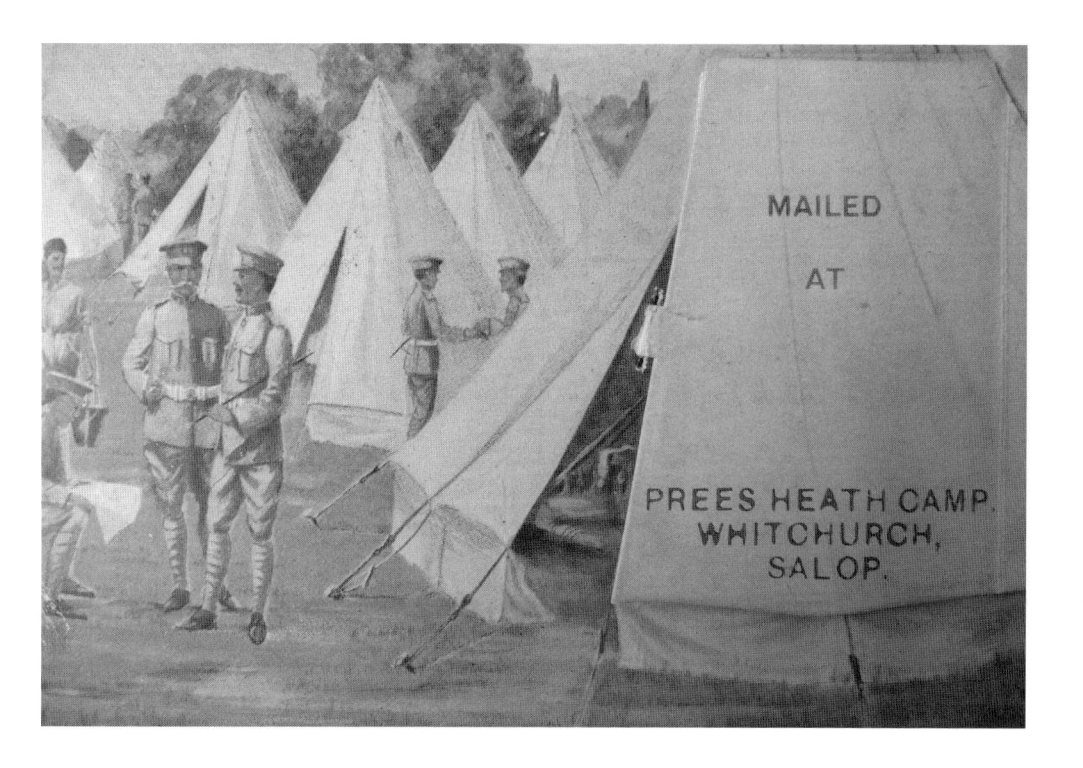

arises they should be seen, why not offer prizes, to stimulate interest still further.'

And by the end of 1916 the one-mile single-track branch line into the camp was taken under the control of Western Command who used it to great effect for transporting troops, supplies and equipment.

In January 1917 a letter of thanks written by Captain Phillips of the Lancashire Fusiliers was sent from Prees Heath to Burnley Football Club thanking them for the gift of a football and jerseys. *'Such occasions as this bring back more than vividly to me the true spirit of the English people. Words are inadequate to express our thanks for the kindness of the supporters of the Club.'*

A fatality at the camp made news in January. A corporal, attending a lesson on explosives with a group of new recruits, had been killed when a number of live detonators, left on a table totally against regulations, had exploded. The corporal died immediately and the verdict returned was death from shock.

In June a recreation room fully equipped with a stage for concerts and entertainments was added to the hospital facilities. The addition was greatly appreciated by the *'gallant men passing through the various wards of the well-appointed hospital'.*

In line with the rest of the country, an outbreak of Spanish flu affected many soldiers towards the end of the year; this was put down to the men's close proximity within the barracks.

In June 1918 a war memorial in the form of a crucifix surrounded by a small garden was erected in the camp outside the Roman Catholic Church of Our Lady of the Trenches and dedicated to the sacred memory, irrespective of their religion, of 'All Officers, Warrant Officers, non-commissioned Officers and men who, after serving on Prees Heath Camp, made the supreme sacrifice for God, King and Empire'. Trumpeters sounded the Last Post and Reveille as troops presented arms and fired three volleys. The troops led by Brigadier General G.W. Dowell CMG, who had unveiled the shrine, then marched past the memorial and saluted.

After the war ended in November the camp was in use as a demobilisation centre with thousands of soldiers passing through its doors before returning to civilian life.

In 1919 Prees Heath was initially retained by the Government with its huts taken down and the common restored to its natural state as had been agreed when it was taken over. It is said that some huts remained, however, and were used for a long time by locals as sheds, workshops and even homes. With the outbreak of the Second World War in 1939 Prees Heath was once again needed, at first as an internment camp for German and Austrian refugees and later, in 1942, as an RAF airfield for bomber training. First known as Whitchurch Heath, by 1943 the area had become known as RAF Tilstock.

After the war both Park Hall and Prees Heath camps were in use as discharge centres in Britain with men arriving from overseas met from their respective stations and marched along the road to the camps singing and whistling old war songs as they anticipated Christmas at home. Countless men 'getting their ticket' passed through the system both day and night as staff worked swiftly to ensure a quick release. A report stated that Park Hall dispersed its men so efficiently that the record for moving a cadet through the system was just twenty minutes, a party of men who arrived at the station at 3.30pm were on the train home by 6.28pm.

At Prees Heath parties of thirty were marched into a hut where Government property in their possession was separated from private belongings. An empty sandbag was provided for the soldier's use to take home any personal items and the Army allowed him to keep his helmet. The men then passed through a succession of huts signing 'Z' forms (required under Government regulations) and were finally given a train ticket to enable them to make their way home. One Tommy, a miner, quipped: *'Well, I've carried a few sandbags out of France and cursed them as I've never cursed anything before, but, hang me, I never thought I should get one as a Christmas present.'*

A suit of clothes was part of the soldiers due, and he could choose from blue, dark brown or dark tweed. Measurements taken, his suit would be forwarded to his home address, alternatively he could take the money returning home with £2 12s 6d in his pocket.

And as the weeks progressed and the huts grew increasingly deserted, life slowly returned to a semblance of normality, although it was to be many years before the effect of the camps on the two towns was forgotten.

CHAPTER 5

1915
U-boats and Zeppelins

At the beginning of 1915, the war to end all wars which should have been over by Christmas still showed no signs of coming to an end, despite the fact that well over a million men had enlisted and been sent overseas.

Britain experienced its first enemy aerial attacks on 19 January 1915. Two German Imperial Navy Zeppelins, sent out with orders to attack Humberside and foiled by bad weather, bombed Great Yarmouth and King's Lynn instead resulting in the deaths of four civilians. An eye-witness described the effect of the raid: *'The whole street seemed to explode, smoke and flames, screams of the dying and wounded, mothers searching frantically for their kids.'*

On 18 February, Germany began its U-boat blockade of the seas surrounding Great Britain declaring the area a war zone. Vessels entering did so at their own risk with attacks taking place without warning on both allied and neutral ships.

Six months of war was taking its toll on the home front, many were suffering ill-health due to stress. Chemists advertised Sanaphos, recommended as a remedy for nervous, mental and physical problems 'caused by the strain of war-time'. It was made by the British Milk Products Company based in London as a replacement for Sanatogen, a nerve tonic previously imported from Germany.

Insurance companies quickly picked up on the menace of the

'danger of infection caused by flies brought back from the battlefield as warmer weather arrived' offering cover against the likelihood. Some even offered Peace Insurance, assuring customers of a pay-out if the war hadn't ended by 1 January or 15 September 1915.

Drunkenness was increasing in Britain in 1915; factory workers earned enough money in two to three days to keep them in drink for a week. Shipbuilding in particular suffered with men on Sunday shifts not turning up for work on Monday. Lloyd George made the comment to the Shipbuilding Federation that Britain was *'fighting Germans, Austrians and drink, and as far as I can see the greatest of these foes is drink'*.

King George V announced he would abstain from alcohol for the duration of the war, urging his people to sign the Patriotic Pledge. *'In order that I may be of the greatest service to my Country at this time of national peril I promise by God's help to abstain from all intoxicants until the end of the war, and to encourage others to do the same.'* The controversial decision taken by Prime Minister Herbert Asquith not to follow the King's example led to damning reports in newspapers.

In April chilling news that poison gas had been used by the Germans at the Second Battle of Ypres did nothing to reassure those at home. It wouldn't be until September during the costly Battle of Loos that Britain retaliated in kind, releasing chlorine gas, which drifted over the German lines with only limited success but was also blown back over the British trenches.

Then on 7 May the passenger ship RMS *Lusitania* was torpedoed by the German U-boat, *U-20*, and sank in just eighteen minutes off the coast of Ireland. The sinking, news of which reached the press in mid-May, resulted in the loss of 1,198 passengers, 128 of whom were American citizens, an incident which no doubt helped to bring America into the conflict.

At midnight on 31 May a Zeppelin air raid on London resulted in seven deaths and caused £18,000 worth of damage. It led to the prompt appearance of posters urging men to 'Join the army at once and help stop an air raid – far better to face the bullets than be killed at home'.

In June the Munitions of War Act brought private companies who supplied the armed forces under the control of the Ministry of Munitions, resulting in no employee being able to leave without the consent of his employer. Permission would not have been granted in any case with all the remaining workforce needed as the war stepped up.

By September column space in newspapers was taken up more and more with reports of heavy losses at the front. Pages of those who had died, were missing, or wounded must have been nervously perused by readers who dreaded to see a name they recognised. Many young couples were marrying in haste too, whilst the groom was on leave. Known as 'khaki weddings', they frequently took place with bridegroom and best man in uniform; after a brief honeymoon the bridegroom would immediately return to the front.

Farmers' Red Cross sales had discovered a novel way of raising money by selling the same animal over and over again at auction, an idea that was repeatedly used as a fundraiser. One report told of a calf being sold forty-five times at one sale before it reached the amazing sum of £69.

In October King George V was appealing for volunteers to sign up:

'At this grave moment in the struggle between my people and a highly organised enemy who has transgressed the Laws of Nations and changed the ordinance that binds civilized Europe together, I appeal to you. The end is not in sight. More men and yet more are wanted to keep my Armies in the Field, to secure Victory and enduring Peace. In ancient days the darkest moment has ever produced in men of our race the sternest resolve. I ask you, men of all classes, to come forward voluntarily and take your share of the fight. You will be giving your support to our brothers, who, for long months, have nobly upheld Britain's past traditions, and the glory of her Arms.'

On 12 October 1915 Nurse Edith Cavell, based in Belgium, was found guilty of treason and sentenced to be shot for harbouring allied soldiers and helping them to escape. Her last words the night before her execution were said to have been *'Patriotism is not enough. I must have no hatred or bitterness towards anyone'*. Her death was quickly used in the press and on posters as a further example of German atrocities. Later in 1920 a memorial was erected in London.

With the end of the year approaching it was reluctantly accepted by all that there was to be no quick answer to the end of the conflict.

Memorial in London to Edith Cavell who was executed by the Germans in October 1915.

Oswestry in 1915

A soldier's letter home gave details of New Year's Eve in the trenches. *'From over the way our "friends" shouted and wished us a Happy New Year and we returned the greetings plus a few small presents,'* it read. The two sides continued calling to each other until New Year's Day dawned at which point hostilities resumed.

At home it was reported that the New Year in Oswestry had been heralded in as usual with a peal of bells from St Oswald's Church and the hooting of buzzers and blowing of whistles from trains on the Cambrian and GWR railways echoing across the town, despite a ban on such activities made law on 8 August 1914 under DORA. Not many people were on the streets although those that were made the effort to do their best to welcome in 1915. In contrast midnight church services had been extremely well-attended particularly by those who had family at the front.

Mr C.C. Rowe, a jeweller in Church Street was displaying a collection of 'curiosities' brought back from the front by a friend who'd been delivering cigarettes and tobacco to the troops. These included a dum-dum bullet, a piece of shrapnel taken from the leg of a soldier, a German helmet, and gruesomely, a piece of a soldier's skull clearly showing the path of a bullet.

The presence of Park Hall Camp was already a godsend for Oswestry tradesmen with J. & R. Baird, Tailors and Outfitters, Oswald Road quickly announcing they stocked officers' service dress and complete equipment. British Warms, an officer's military greatcoat designed to be worn over a uniform, could be purchased for 73s, trousers for 16s 6d or 21s, all items made to measure.

On 8 and 13 January Oswestry's vicar, the Reverend Lutener, and his wife invited local Pals currently on leave, together with their lady friends, to a dance at Church House. For these auspicious occasions Mrs Campbell of nearby Broom Hall loaned plants to decorate the stage. The vicar told the gathering how proud the people of Oswestry were of the Pals and the part they had played so far in the crisis. He finished by saying that he hoped before long the town would have the opportunity of giving them all a rousing welcome home.

A report on the hardships the Belgian family of Monsieur and Madame Baenckaerts had experienced appeared in January. Walking from their home to the Dutch frontier, they had slept in fields before finally leaving Holland for Britain. All their money, £80, approximately £3,760 today, had by then been used up.

At the beginning of the year shortage of labour on farms was beginning to have a serious effect. One local solution suggested was that children should leave school early and be put to work. Controversially it was recorded that *'farmers did not want the sharp children, but the dull ones, who would never learn anything in school after twelve years of age.'*

Six months into the war the removal of so many horses from the countryside was very noticeable. Half a million animals had been commandeered by the military since war commenced, supplementing the 25,000 horses owned by the British Army; thousands had come from farms, an industry much dependent on horsepower.

Mrs Campbell of Broom Hall, in conjunction with the Royal Society for the Prevention of Cruelty to Animals (RSPCA), was appealing for funds for 'our dumb allies', horses currently engaged with forces overseas in France. *'Hundreds are sick and wounded and housed in veterinary hospitals, I am sure that many in Oswestry and the surrounding area would be glad of an opportunity to ease the animals' suffering,'* she wrote.

With the impending arrival of hundreds of men for military training at Park Hall Camp, morality patrols undertaken by women were being discussed by the War Relief Committee, the idea meeting with some scepticism. Later in the year the Home Secretary, Reginald McKenna, authorised a recruitment scheme for women police officers with over 1,000 women signing up in the first week.

Sport played a large part in boosting morale for both civilians and military throughout the war, with regular football fixtures and boxing and cricket matches taking place between the troops and civilians. Oswestry Amateur Swimming Club was delighted when a number of ladies joined them, not wanting to see the club suffer due to lack of members. Looked upon as a patriotic move, seven were immediately co-opted onto the committee to replace men who had left to fight.

On 24 April Oswestry Social Service League was looking for women and girls to train in light farm work at Harper Adams Agricultural College situated some forty miles from the town. The appeal initially had a nil response with one local farmer commenting that he *'did not wonder at it, some of the farm work was hard even for* him, it was very laborious, planting potatoes on farms, and it was work that women ought not to be called upon to do'.

Oswestry Education Committee was concerned by the decrease in boys' attendance at afternoon school. It was discovered that the youngsters were working, either for tradesmen or at Park Hall Camp. This did not please the chairman who felt that many children were already seriously lacking in their education leading to boys being *'in danger of turning into wastrels and idlers'*.

In May 1915 a letter to the *Advertizer* commented on the large number of women frequenting public houses in Oswestry. A disapproving writer signing himself A Moderate Drinker wrote: *'Money spent on liquor would be better off in the pockets of local businesses that are under duress. Shut down half the public houses and close the rest at 6pm. This will not happen of course, as the Town Council would be afraid of losing votes.'*

The *Lusitania* incident led to an increase in anti-German riots throughout Britain, with shops destroyed and burnt to the ground and people driven from their homes. Oswestry was praised for not participating in such demonstrations. *'It would only increase the anxiety of the Government and the local authorities, withdraw the military from their proper functions, and cast a serious expense upon ratepayers at a time when every additional penny of public expenditure puts a fresh strain upon our nation's resources,'* was the opinion in Oswestry.

Towards the middle of the year questions were being asked concerning those who had still to join up. One man wrote:

'There are many sons of farmers and many shop assistants who have not joined, their conduct to me seems unutterably mean, they should be shunned as lepers and cowards and outcasts of society.

The general opinion seems to be that they would "go when fetched". The Government should announce their intention to institute powers to fetch "these slackers" after a certain date, which might have an immediate effect on recruitment.'

His remarks pre-empted the introduction in August of the National Registration Act which would record everyone who was eligible for military service for future reference.

In late May the need for further recreational facilities was recognised. At the monthly meeting of the Oswestry Social Service League Mr E. Rowlands, district head of the YMCA, addressed the committee, explaining that shortly 22,000 men would be stationed at Park Hall Camp and Oswestry was the only place where soldiers could come each evening, except for Saturdays when they were allowed to travel to Wrexham or Shrewsbury. Requesting that three YMCA centres where soldiers could pass their time in 'innocent pleasure and amusement' be set up in the town to supplement those in the camp, he also appealed for male and female volunteers to help in both locations. The vicar quickly assured Mr Rowlands that Oswestry ladies could most certainly help but only from 10am until 5pm at the camp, not considering it wise for them to be there after that time.

The thought of thousands of men pouring into Oswestry looking for entertainment must have shaken the organisers of the meeting who continued to discuss further social programmes including the erection of a hut in Cae Glas Park capable of accommodating 2,000 to 3,000 men.

Soldiers bringing their sweethearts to entertainments in the town found support from the Reverend J.J. Poyner. *'Under proper supervision'*, he said, *'it was something that would make the interchange of friendship between the sexes convenient and allowable.'* Somewhat firmly he added that was his opinion and he did not care who knew it, obviously expecting opposition from others to his proposal. His retort may have been triggered by reports of lowered morality in areas where troops were billeted, although whether it was the soldiers or the girls who were responsible was unclear.

Promptly a letter appeared defending the soldiers.

'Now, about young girls. Tommy is not to be blamed; most of the girls force their company upon the chaps. I recall seeing young girls and women waiting for chaps to come out at 5.30pm in Bexhill-on-Sea. Do try to prevent this kind of thing, servant girls were not allowed out after 6.30pm in Bexhill, if the ladies of Oswestry do the same there will not be so many cases. Keep Tommy amused, and then you will find that he will give you no trouble whatever.'

A letter from girls who had *'the pluck to defend themselves from slander'* quickly arrived:

> *'Our girls would hardly think of giving as much as a glance at the soldiers (so called) camping in our districts, after the cases we read and hear of, we know there are good and bad amongst the soldiers, and the good and those on active service are a credit to their country. It is regrettable that girls have to stand being slandered by being regarded as "all the same" when it is evident they are not.'*

News that the Royal Circus and Menagerie of Lord John Sanger and Sons would soon be in town must have come as a welcome relief for all, something to take their minds off the grim news from abroad. The talents of eight French clowns, ponies performing musical chairs, and a giant horse called Goliath partnered with the smallest pony in the world would entertain. A team of elephants would dine, fight and play in a band whilst the Aerial Danes would give an exhibition as human flying machines, all for admission prices ranging from 6d to 3s.

At the start of July W.H. Thomas and Sons, Salop Road who supplied horseshoe boxes to the Government, supplemented their boy labour with a number of public schoolgirls who had volunteered to fill places in both the workshop and on the staff. Despite being unaccustomed to manual labour, the girls, who donated their pay of 2d an hour to the War Fund, were reported as doing their tasks in an efficient manner.

The town was in the forefront when classes on making munitions were offered by Oswestry Education Committee in late July. In conjunction with the Liverpool Munitions Committee, volunteers were trained in rough turning, the material worked then shaped into shells. A report in September confirmed that sixty-five males and several females had joined, twenty-four since being sent on to work in Birmingham and Liverpool factories.

Although it was slow progress, some farmers were beginning to acknowledge women's agricultural skills. The idea by the farming community that a woman ploughing was absurd had quickly been dismissed by reports of women doing just that in Belgium and France. It was felt that with a good physique and intelligence, there would be no problem if farmers would only undertake to train them. Meanwhile, with late summer approaching the Army Council was offering soldiers for hire to deal with the hay harvest. To a certain extent labour problems were solved later in 1915 when children from the workhouse over twelve years of age were boarded out at farms to undertake work previously done by men. The children should also have attended classes in the evening, one farmer commenting he doubted they would be fit enough after working all day.

National Egg Collection for the Wounded month took place in August 1915. The initial aim was to collect one million eggs for use by injured men arriving home, as well as shipping some abroad to soldiers in France and Flanders. Mrs Venables in Oswestry and Mrs Dugdale in Whitchurch were two of the collectors situated in local markets throughout Shropshire for any donations. In Shropshire alone Red Cross volunteers regularly collected between 53,000 and 71,000 eggs every year until hostilities ceased.

In between bulletins from abroad local news continued to be reported. In August a fire at a Llansilin farm some six and a half miles from Oswestry was no doubt read with a variety of emotions. Oswestry fire brigade had been ready in minutes but neither trotting horses nor motor tractors could be found to pull the engine. Finally two Corporation carthorses were harnessed up with the firemen instructed to walk beside them. Two hours later, slow progress having been made over the steep roads leading to the farm, the brigade finally arrived but by then the barn and haystack were no more.

Some 2,000 people gathered on Bailey Head on 11 August to mark the anniversary of the declaration of war in 1914. A military band played rousing music before the National Anthem was sung with passion. This eagerness to commemorate the anniversary of war breaking out diminished in the coming years as the conflict dragged on indefinitely.

Mr Wally George was keeping up the spirits of civilians and troops alike at the Oswestry Playhouse, regularly offering a variety of entertainments. In autumn 1915 he presented 'Her Luck in London' a dramatic film followed later in the week by 'The Fatal Woman'. By the end of the week the world-renowned novelty gymnasts act 'Bouncing Dillons' were appearing. *'Bouncing competitions will be held at every performance,'* announced Mr George, *'and there will assuredly be great fun to be had.'*

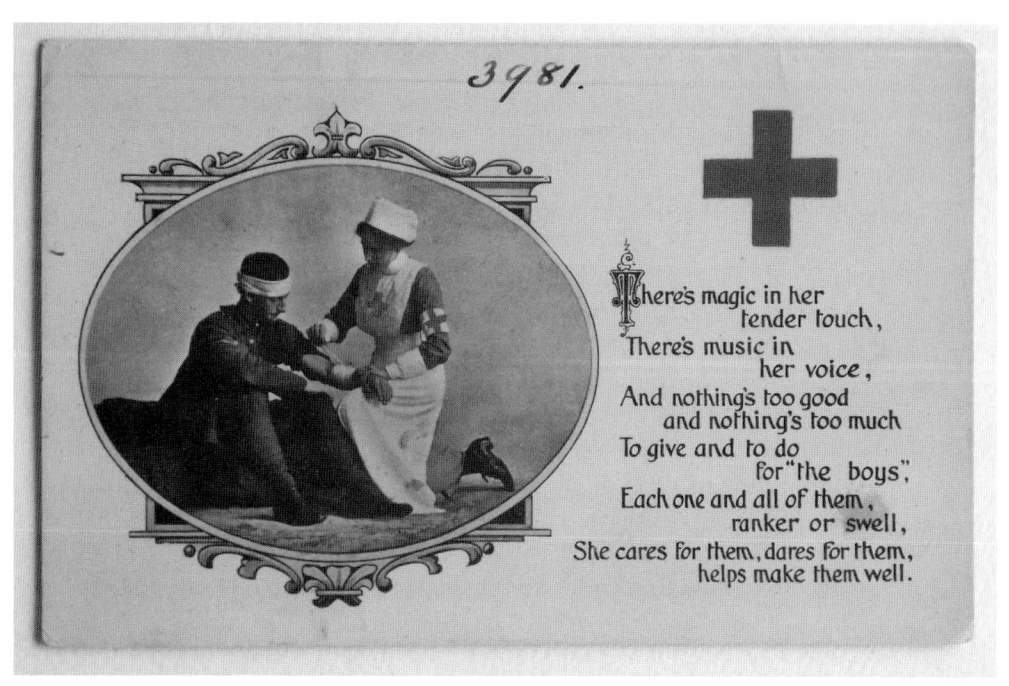

> There's magic in her tender touch,
> There's music in her voice,
> And nothing's too good and nothing's too much
> To give and to do for "the boys",
> Each one and all of them, ranker or swell,
> She cares for them, dares for them, helps make them well.

A British Red Cross nurse tends a wounded soldier.

On 7 December 1915 Ardmillan House, situated at the top of Shelf Bank overlooking Oswestry and the railway station, was lent by its owner, Ann Thomas, for use as an auxiliary military hospital. This was in line with many large houses throughout the country urgently requisitioned as hospitals due to the numbers of returning wounded. Six wards with five beds each, a surgery, day rooms and mess room were created and staffed by a British Red Cross sister, two nurses and six VADs. In the summer wards were supplemented by tents in the garden housing another sixteen beds. Throughout the course of the war Ardmillan Auxiliary Hospital was well supported by local people with frequent entertainments and dances held to raise funds.

With Christmas approaching Hobley's Tea Rooms were advertising their Famous Selections for parcels to France. Contents included plum puddings in special tin moulds to comply with War Office Regulations, Christmas crackers and cakes with patriotic designs. Assuring customers that an assortment of Tommy's favourite goods bought from the shop would be packed expertly for shipping overseas their advertisement ends, *'Just imagine his smile of delight on receipt of a parcel from home.'*

Whitchurch 1915
At the beginning of January a letter sent to a Whitchurch resident gave an idea of the conditions the KSLI were experiencing. *'It is simply awful out here,'* writes Lieutenant Smith, *'bitterly cold with mud over our boot tops and the fellows in the trenches knee deep in water and clay. Christmas gifts are just beginning to arrive, what a generous public we have to have the comfort of Tommy so much at heart.'*

Farmers in the Whitchurch area were experiencing great difficulty in obtaining labour early in the year, many of the young men previously employed having left for the front or employed at Prees Heath Camp. Recent violent storms had caused considerable damage with acres of grassland under water further depressing farmers who were desperately trying to improve their output with reduced manpower.

In January the *Herald* was happy to confirm that things were looking up in Whitchurch as another twelve men headed for the front bringing the total enlisting within the month to thirty-six. So far the bulk of men enlisting had been attached to the Army Service Corps (ASC) others joining the KSLI and the Royal Army Medical Corps (RAMC).

In mid-January the pantomime Mother Hubbard was performed in the Town Hall with all proceeds donated to the Cottage Hospital and local refugee funds courtesy of the promoter Mr Rutter. With tickets sold out for both performances, it made a welcome change for all.

Broughall Cottage, taken over as an Auxiliary Hospital at the start of the war with beds for twenty patients and two trained nurses, received eight soldiers suffering from wounds, rheumatism and frostbite early in February with ten more expected very shortly; these numbers increased considerably as the years passed. A party of injured Belgian soldiers joined their refugee countrymen in the town in mid-January having been brought in from a local hospital to enjoy a picture show. One of the soldiers, despite having been shot in the legs and abdomen was the life and soul of the party. *'I have shot nine and am going back to shoot ninety,'* he declared enthusiastically.

In February a patriotic concert in the Town Hall was raising funds for the YMCA now established at Prees Heath Camp. Noted artistes took part with songs performed by the Wesleyan Choir. The concert ended with young boys marching forward with the national flags of each country whilst the audience sang the appropriate National

Anthem. Three Belgian boys evacuated to Whitchurch were chosen to carry their country's flag.

In March Whitchurch Urban District Council reported that the swimming and slipper baths in the town would be open to soldiers in uniform at a charge of 1d each, with free use of the Market Hall and Corn Exchange for soldiers' entertainments also available, provided all damage and out of pocket expenses were made good. What were they expecting!

The Town Hall cinema was seeing plenty of customers from Prees Heath Camp with Mr Pendleton, the proprietor, showing a variety of programmes. Great disappointment had been expressed when the men found there was a ban on smoking but they were quickly assured that moves were being made to allow it on future occasions.

A church parade took place in the town in May with over 1,000 men marching through the streets preceded by the bagpipes. After a sermon in St Alkmund's Parish Church the men returned along a High Street lined with cheering crowds to meet with detachments of men who had attended services elsewhere. Tea for the soldiers was provided in private homes, Church House and the Congregational Schoolroom. By

High Street, Whitchurch, where crowds gathered in their hundreds to cheer on the troops after a Church Parade.

Men out on the town from Prees Heath Camp, Whitchurch. (courtesy of Peter Lea)

March residents of Whitchurch and the surrounding areas, under the heading PATRIOTIC WHITCHURCH, were being praised by the press for the enthusiastic welcome they had extended to the 4,000 to 5,000 men already encamped nearby at Prees Heath. It was anticipated that eventually 10,000 to 15,000 men would take up residence. On hearing of this, Whitchurch people were quick to form a committee to ensure that suitable entertainment would be readily available.

With the outbreak of war Egerton Drill Hall, built in 1898 and formerly used by the Territorials, had immediately been handed over by its trustees. Newly decorated and furnished, paid for by subscriptions from the townspeople and a generous subscription from Mr W.H. Smith, a local businessman with much influence in the town, it had been transformed offering a reading and recreation room where any man in uniform was able to relax and obtain refreshments. The hall was formally opened by Whitchurch officials and members of the army hierarchy to the accompaniment of the pipers and drummers of the 16th Highland Light Infantry.

A runaway horse pulling a hay cart made the news in April; it had galloped down Green End towards the Bull Ring scattering hay in all directions and totally destroying a jeweller's shop window. Reaching the Bull Ring, the horse's mad dash was brought to an end and luckily no-one was injured.

Broughall Auxiliary Hospital staged a concert for wounded soldiers in May; amongst the acts was Mr Jesse Hearne whose attendance had been secured by organiser Mr E. Jones. His speciality, 'whistling and balancing feats', was said to have been particularly appreciated by the patients, who applauded loudly.

In May an announcement that Whitchurch Cricket Club was abandoning its fixtures for the season disappointed some. The club however, would organize matches for the benefit of the soldiers as they understood *'there were some very good players amongst both officers and men with every prospect of some excellent matches being arranged.'* Before long the first knock-out matches were taking place, soldiers admitted free, civilians charged 2d.

Sir Wyndham Hanmer of Bettisfield Park was once again appealing for men to come forward in a letter to the *Herald* in May. Detailing Kitchener's call for 300,000 more men for the army he wrote:

> *'Active service is not for all of us but we can put our shoulder to the wheel in our daily occupations, older men and those who are ineligible for the army can serve their country by taking over a younger man's post thus releasing him for service.'*

Green End, Whitchurch.

He finishes by appealing that men still at home come forward and show their grit. *'Don't let us wait for so degrading a term as conscription,'* he pleads.

Troops currently finishing training who shortly would be leaving for the front had gained both the respect and friendship of Whitchurch civilians over the six weeks they had been billeted in the camp. On the evening of their departure almost the whole of the town turned out to give them a hearty send off. The soldiers were said to be in excellent spirits singing and cheering as they marched through the streets and on arrival at the station calling for three cheers for Whitchurch.

Sergeant Frith, a veteran of the Boer War and a former resident from Green End who had emigrated to Canada before returning to fight for his mother country, was convalescing in Whitchurch after suffering the effects of gas in the trenches. He commented that, in his opinion the war in South Africa had been mere child's play compared to the present gigantic struggle but he was confident of the allies' victory in the long run and was looking forward to returning to the front.

At the beginning of July a rally took place in Whitchurch and district run by the county recruiting authorities. The band of the KSLI paraded through the town during the afternoon, preceding an evening meeting held in the Market Hall. Here, the Reverend F.H. Wilson recently returned from the front, appealed to all men who were able to join up to do so, not only to take up arms for their king and country but also for their God. Mr W.H. Smith, local businessman, urged anyone who had influence and knew of a young man who was hesitating to encourage him to enlist without delay. Speaking of the previous week's victorious battles he was proud to say that the Shropshires had distinguished themselves significantly being at the very front of the push.

At the beginning of August a labourer drinking at a public house in the town took exception to a private from Prees Heath Camp, knocking him down and kicking him on the jaw until he was unconscious. With the arrival of the Military Police, a corporal chased the labourer who nevertheless escaped into the town's maze of streets. The soldier was taken to the Cottage Hospital from whence he returned to Prees Heath Camp later in the evening.

Towards midnight in the vicinity of Raven's Yard, Watergate Street where the labourer lived, military personnel in the area were attacked by women hurling stones. Four soldiers received injuries, one seriously, and it wasn't until their sergeant ordered his troops to fix bayonets on the aggressive crowd and the police arrived on the scene, that the yard was cleared.

At the Court Sessions the labourer was charged with being drunk and disorderly and with assaulting a private in the 17th (Service) Battalion of the Welsh Regiment, a bantam battalion, stationed at Prees Heath Camp. When asked how the incident had developed the labourer accused the military of kicking him but was nevertheless sent to gaol for ten weeks with hard labour.

In August an extremely successful Red Cross Sale took place in Whitchurch in association with the farmer community. Presided over by local auctioneers Frank Lloyd and Henry Manley, the auction in the Town Hall consisted of livestock, cheese, poultry, dairy produce and useful miscellaneous effects. In three and a half hours, during which time the auctioneers repeatedly made sure that farmers understood their patriotic duty, a sum of £350 was raised, a supreme effort equating to over £16,000 in today's values (the relative value of £1 in 1914 equals approximately £48 today) with one cheese selling for £12 19s whilst a lamb reached a price of £42. At the same time young girls were out on the streets urging all to donate to the fund which by the end of the day raised nearly £650.

After the auction Captain Beville Stanier MP took over the platform vacated by the auctioneers and appealed to those who had not yet joined the colours to do so. *'It is the duty of all men who are capable to see to it they wear a uniform,'* he told them pointing out the gravity of the situation in Europe before commenting on the fact that he understood that at one time the Volunteers had been looked down on, now however, it was not only Kitchener but also the king who were asking for the force to be strengthened.

'The Volunteer movement is now established in Shropshire and I appeal to Whitchurch men to do their part in connection with it. The town is at present the only one in Shropshire which has not yet taken up the movement and I appeal to men to come forward and form a battalion,' he urged, finishing his speech by asking for someone to come forward and organise the setting up of a force.

In defence of Whitchurch one member at the meeting was anxious to point out that the town had always done its fair share in the past and now they were told that it was their duty to establish a Volunteer Force in the town he was sure it would be done. A Volunteer Force had been formed some time back but for some reason discontinued, but he was certain after hearing the appeal from Captain Stanier that the men of Whitchurch would soon re-form and would not shrink from their duty.

In September the sad news that Miss E.J. Morrey, assistant mistress at nearby Prees School for sixteen years had been drowned on her way to meet her fiancé in Canada reached Whitchurch. The Royal Mail Ship *Hesperian* had been torpedoed on the night of 4 September 1915 and although Miss Morrey had reached a lifeboat, together with thirty-two other survivors she lost her life when it capsized as it was being lowered. She had been urged to wait before sailing because of the danger of being torpedoed by German submarines but had commented *'they won't torpedo the boat I am going to travel in. I am not a bit afraid'*.

In early November Pat Collins' High-Class Amusements were once again visiting Whitchurch, this time to give a benefit night for Whitchurch Cottage Hospital and Broughall Auxiliary Hospital. The event was well supported raising substantial funds which were much welcomed by the nursing staff.

And as Christmas approached Adela Dugdale from nearby Terrick Hall, was appealing for Christmas fare for the Shropshire Yeomanry.

'We shall be most grateful for pheasants, dressed poultry, ham, cheese and plum puddings. All contributions to be taken to my home not later than 17 December.' She finishes by saying the fact their Christmas dinner had come from home would add enormously to the enjoyment of it by the soldiers.

Special Gifts for Soldiers was also the aim of the Whitchurch Entertaining Committee who had invited men in the services to attend the Drill Hall and Corn Exchange for a Christmas meal. The request for gifts of dessert oranges, crackers, and mince pies was responded to enthusiastically ensuring Christmas Day for the Tommies would be successful.

Recruitment in the town saw a surge mid December due to constant streams of men of all classes wishing to be sworn in under Lord Derby's Scheme B. The scheme signified a man's willingness to go to the front if needed but did not include 'starred' men, those in an essential occupation.

As 1915 drew to a close it seemed that victory for the Allies was still a long way off. Nevertheless, parcels were sent with heartfelt wishes for a happy Christmas to loved ones overseas and in return, beautifully embroidered patriotic Christmas cards with cheerful messages were received from those serving on the Western Front. In those dark times the cards must have been a glimmer of hope; at least it meant that their men were still alive.

A beautifully embroidered Christmas Card 'Britons All' sent from the front.

CHAPTER 6

1916
The Year of the Somme

❖

With the introduction of the Military Services Act in January 1916 voluntary enlistment came to an end. From 2 March men aged between eighteen and forty-one were likely to be called up to join the army unless married, widowed with children, in the service of the Royal Navy, a religious minister or working in a reserved occupation. By the 25 March the Act had been extended to include married men.

Military Service Tribunals were soon hearing applications for exemption from conscription, mostly from men who were medically unfit, doing work of national importance or where hardship would be caused. Only about two per cent of the exemption cases put forward involved conscientious objectors.

Britain experienced severe weather with snowstorms and strong winds affecting many parts of the country in March 1916. Hilly areas in Shropshire saw the heaviest falls for over forty years and with mines closed, people were breaking up furniture to use as fuel. Even funerals were proving difficult to arrange with roads leading to churches and graveyards having to be cleared of snowdrifts before burials could take place.

On 24 April, whilst Britain and its allies were preoccupied with their enemies overseas, the Easter Rising took place in Dublin, the aim being to end British rule and establish an Irish Republic. The rebellion lasted six days and before it ended on 29 April, 450 had been killed and 3,000 wounded.

Monday, 24 April was also the day chosen by the German navy to bombard Great Yarmouth, a British Navy submarine base on the east coast, and Lowestoft, a base for mine laying and sweeping. This strategic move was designed to bring British forces into battle whilst the Germans were in the best position to retaliate.

On 21 May 1916 the Government introduced the British Summer Time Act, brought in as a daylight saving measure to save both fuel and money. The Act has never been repealed and remains in force to this day.

In June a shocked nation learnt that Lord Kitchener, Secretary of State for War, together with members of his staff, had been drowned on the way to Russia along with other passengers and crew on HMS *Hampshire*. The ship had been sailing west of the Orkneys when it struck a mine and, with strong winds and heavy seas running at the time, although four boats had been lowered, only twelve survivors were found. On 6 July David Lloyd George was appointed Secretary of State for War in Kitchener's place.

At the beginning of July reports of the disastrous outcome of the first day of the Battle of the Somme reached those at home. The Allies had suffered catastrophic losses with whole units wiped out and almost 20,000 British soldiers slaughtered.

Before long another concern was raising its head, this time at home. In 1916 there had been a lower than usual yield from the wheat harvest and, linked with failures in potato crops, shortages were inevitable. As a result food prices were rising rapidly with some essential provisions too expensive to buy for many.

The August Bank Holiday did not take place to prevent a repeat of the Easter holidays when troop trains had been cancelled in favour of holidaymakers. Despite the fact that Britain was in the middle of a bitter war, some still complained of loss of trade due to the decision. It was hard to believe in view of the serious situation, but the realities of war were brought home later in the month when cinemas were showing the film 'The Battle of the Somme'. The most poignant part was footage of a soldier carrying a dying comrade on his back. Seeing the appalling conditions at the front must have instilled real fear for families in the audiences.

In early September Lieutenant Leefe Robinson of the 39th Home Guard Squadron, flying a BE2c aircraft, brought down a German

1916 THE YEAR OF THE SOMME 85

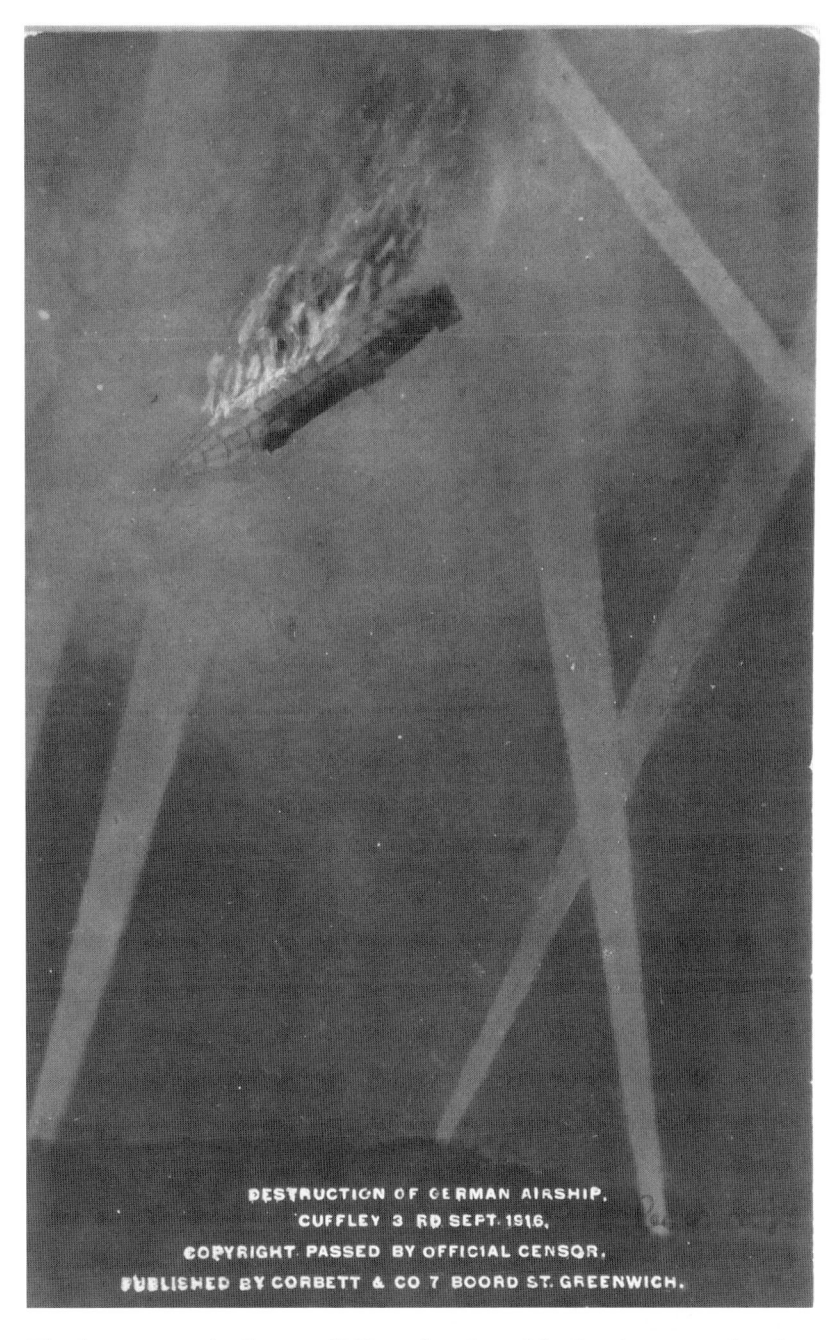

The destruction of a German SL11 airship. Bound for London it was shot down at Cuffley, Hertfordshire on 3 September 1916.

A British tank on display. Tanks toured Britain to encourage the buying of War Bonds and Savings Certificates.

airship, the S-11 in Cuffley, Herfordshire for which he was awarded the Victoria Cross. The first enemy airship to be shot down on British soil, its demise was witnessed by a jubilant crowd who sang the national anthem and cheered as it descended in flames, killing its fifteen man crew. It didn't take long for the British Government to seize upon the incident, using it for propaganda purposes.

Britain learnt on 15 September that a new weapon had entered the theatre of war when thirty-six tanks were sent out to attack the enemy on the Somme. Tanks had been in the development stage for some time with Winston Churchill, who had founded the Landships Committee in February 1915 to investigate troop transporters, a firm supporter. Weighing thirty tons, each tank had a crew of eight, was fitted with heavy guns and had a top speed of four miles per hour. Later some tanks were displayed around towns and cities to encourage the buying of War Bonds and Savings Certificates.

Despite heavy driving rain turning the Somme battlegrounds into swamps in October the fighting continued and it wasn't until 8 November that hostilities ended, the Allies having advanced just six miles into German territory. Four months of bitter warfare had resulted in 420,000 British, 195,000 French and 650,000 German casualties.

By 22 December the Ministries of Food, Labour, Pensions and Shipping were in place to cope with increasing difficulties on the home front although panic food buying had calmed down and limited supplies were available. Wasting any food was looked upon as a crime and fines were levelled even for those discovered feeding pigeons or wild animals.

Oswestry in 1916
In Oswestry, a letter sent from Edward Edwards serving with the Royal Field Artillery (RFA) and previously employed as a wheelwright at the works of Messrs Rogers and Son, described in detail Christmas and New Year's Eve in the trenches at the end of 1915.

> *'After tea on Christmas Eve, we were having a game of cards in our dug-out (everything had been very quiet all day till then), when the enemy started throwing Christmas boxes over in the shape of shells. About fifty dropped around us, and then we let them have it. Our four guns were busy until midnight, and then everything became quiet again; so we just pulled our boots off and laid down for a sleep, which we very much needed.*
>
> *About two o'clock they sent some gas over, so we had to put our gas helmets on 'til it cleared off. After the gas attack, the Germans made a rush out of their trenches. Our Infantry however, let them come half way and then opened fire on them, wiping them down like hailstones.*
>
> *Christmas Day was very quiet about here; but we could hear an artillery duel at Ypres all day. I daresay you wonder what sort of a feed we had. Well, we had two biscuits and a rasher of bacon and half a pint of tea for breakfast, a small piece of pork, two spuds and a small piece of pudding and half a pint of beer for dinner, and a sing song after. The cooks got merry after dinner; consequently, we got no tea at all.*
>
> *On New Year's Eve we were bombarding all night till dawn. An infantry chap told me in the morning that the RFA Band was at Armentieres. Being a cornet player, I took French leave all day and enjoyed myself a treat.*

Well how are the Pals going on by now? Are they out here yet? We are starting leave so I am expecting to be home before long. I heard that the Oswestry Pals used to get cigs sent them from England. I have been in the Army thirteen months and been out here four months and I have never had any sent me. I suppose that is because I am with the eighteen-pounder gun, and people think I don't want any.'

Oswestry man Private J.H. Pendry at the beginning of February sent home a 'Carol of the Trenches' sung to the tune of 'Hark the Herald Angels Sing':

Hark we hear the bullets ping,
Defiance to the German King.
Send some more and make us smile,
For we will not reconcile.
Joyful all ye nations rise,
Confound the Kaiser for his lies.
We will loudly shout and sing,
Down, for aye, the German King.
Hark, we hear the bullets ping
Defiance to the German King.

We will sing with one accord,
Actions brave we will applaud,
With happy thoughts of days to come,
When we are safely back at home,
In khaki decked, the damsels see,
Rejoice again in unity;
Pleased again with them to dwell,
These our thoughts on sentinel.
Hark, we hear the bullets ping
Defiance to the German King.

Hail the day that brings us peace,
Hail the day when conflicts cease.
Light and life, and all it brings,
Joy throughout the trenches rings.

Then we all shall loudly cry,
There's good health until we die,
And happiness may crown the earth,
Once more express our joyful mirth;
Then no more shall bullets ping,
Glory to our sovereign King.

No doubt Private Pendry echoed the thoughts of many soldiers shivering in the trenches Christmas 1915, particularly the last verse.

The increasing numbers of wounded and sick men returning from the front were keeping Red Cross trains busy transferring patients to hospitals throughout the country. In Oswestry on 9 January news was received that seventy wounded soldiers had been transported into Shrewsbury Station. *'Needless to add, none were sent to Oswestry,'* said one local report. *'Our town, in spite of its waiting hospital, is apparently still regarded as too inaccessible by the authorities.'*

Back home there was plenty of entertainment to shorten a cold January and distract thoughts from what was taking place abroad. With all monies received going to Ardmillan Auxiliary Hospital, St Oswald's Church Institute held a 'Cinderella Dance' in the Victoria Rooms on 17 January, the well-known Mr Tims' Band providing the music, tickets modestly priced at 1s. This was followed by a Leap Year Ball organised for 20 January at the same venue tickets priced at 2s. Meanwhile Mr Wally George, proprietor of the Playhouse in Oswestry, was presenting the Royal Scarlet Entertainments twice nightly at 7pm and 9pm. *'Important and Expensive Engagement,'* his advertisement trumpeted, *'of the Famous in Burlesque Concerts, Trios, Duets and Dancing – all this for just 1s, 9d, 6d and 3d.'*

New industries, as a result of the war, were springing up to meet demand from the military. Cambrian Railway Company, aware of the opportunities, ran an advertisement offering a number of suitable building sites, all supplied with water for generating motive power and all ready immediately for the erection of works, factories, and warehouses with siding connections to the railway.

The pressing need for more men to join the forces was news yet again early in 1916. In Oswestry few had presented themselves at the recruitment office to register under the voluntary scheme introduced in 1915 by Lord Derby, Director General of Recruiting. The scheme, which stipulated that married men would only be called up once all single men had been taken, was abandoned when the Military Service Act was introduced and conscription for unmarried men began.

At the end of February Mrs Swann, Commandant at Ardmillan Auxiliary Hospital confirmed that five convalescent patients would shortly be arriving from the Royal Salop Infirmary. On the day a crowd gathered on Shelf Bank close to Ardmillan to witness the patients' arrival, the report in the *Advertiser* on 9 January lamenting non-use of the hospital must have had some effect; it had its first patients.

At the beginning of March under the headline WOMEN ON THE LAND the *Advertiser* was championing women's ability to undertake work previously done by men.

> *'The great difficulty facing those who are organising the effort is not so much that of securing the necessary women but of overcoming the prejudice of many farmers against accepting their services. The farmer often regards the lady volunteer as a mere amateur and we have heard of a farmer who told his local Tribunal last week that he tried a woman at the plough and "she took a cushion to sit on and a parasol to hold over her!"'*

The congregation attending the Oswald Road Presbyterian Church had a lucky escape on 20 February. Shortly after they'd left, a huge block of sandstone fell from the top of the building landing with a terrific crash on the steps of the church porch. With Zeppelin attacks in January 1915 still very much on people's minds the newspaper headline ALARMING MISHAP AT OSWESTRY – NOT A ZEPPELIN BOMB confirmed the first thoughts of the parishioners. If they had left ten minutes later, none would have been alive to tell the tale.

In late February Private W.H. Lewis wrote to his family thanking them for a parcel of comforts he had received.

> *'We have lost a lot of lads that came out with me,'* he writes. *'I have not seen Gardner for two weeks. Tell George Thompson I have seen his son Jack. He is all right and looks well. I should like to find Percy Phillip's grave. He lies buried where we now are; but there are so many all over the place and those that have*

money and come out here after the war will see some sights. They say the Germans are bringing up the bigger guns on our front.

I wish it was all over, it is awful. We have had a lot of snow here; it has been snowing all the week, and it must be very bad in the trenches.'

Sadly Private Lewis, formerly an engine driver with the Cambrian Railway, fell in action on 10 March 1916.

At home an announcement that due to war lighting regulations all lamps would have to be shaded and extinguished entirely by 11pm except for those considered necessary by the police did nothing to encourage the local populace to venture out at night. This became evident on March Fair Day. Usually a crowded event with both business and pleasurable pursuits taking place, it received poor attendance and although a number of shows and shooting galleries were present on the Recreation Ground few were there to enjoy the entertainment. Lack of good lighting coupled with particularly cold, wintry weather was blamed.

By mid March the Oswestry Traders' Association was discussing early closing times in shops due to lighting restrictions. A heated debate took place with a variety of different times proposed, the mayor doing his very best to get the attendees to come to a decision. Finally, the mayor's patience exhausted, it was decided to leave it to a committee to sort out the problem.

By early April a decision had been made, a letter appearing in the *Advertizer* addressed to the mayor read:

'Sir, the Oswestry Traders' Association appreciate greatly the support you gave to the idea of earlier closing in the town, and as the traders now have to engage young ladies to take the places of the young men who have left to join the Colours, they hope the public will do all they can to make their duties easier by shopping early as having to stand for long hours at a stretch is very trying for lady assistants.'

Oswestry Borough Tribunal was receiving increasing numbers of appeals for exemption after the introduction of the Military Services

Act earlier in the year. An Oswestry grocer appealed for exemption for his 19-year-old son who managed Park Hall Camp canteen.

> *'What does your son do as a canteen manager,'* he was asked.
> *'His business is to order stores for the military,'* was the reply.
> *'This canteen is practically a branch of your shop?'*
> *'Yes.'*
> *'Then you can do without it. You have two shops in Oswestry, close one and keep on the other. My opinion is that no civilian of military age ought to be employed in a camp; you are running this canteen for your own profit?'*
> *'Oh yes, that is so,'* came the reply.
> The verdict was instant, *'Your appeal is disallowed.'*

Appearing in increasing numbers at the beginning of May as the growing season approached, were farmers pleading for exclusion from call-up for their sons. When asked if they had tried taking on women or seeking help at the Labour Exchange most answered no, one individual asking why the Labour Exchange hadn't come to him.

Despite businesses and factories in towns and cities accepting women workers in a wide range of occupations, take-up in the country was still painfully slow. A surprising number of reasons were given for why women couldn't be used; one local farmer was reluctant as he considered it *'would kill some of them and injure others'*. To be fair, women themselves were not always keen to take up manual work, some thought it degrading, with one group employed to spread manure on fields being so taunted and ridiculed by their neighbours they had given up.

A farmer appealed for his son at a May tribunal as he had been unable to get another man to replace him. The military representative at the meeting enquired *'have you tried to get women labour?'* The farmer was scornful. *'No,'* he replied.

The chairman was cold in his reply. *'So many of you never try, and you laugh at the idea of employing women. Your application is refused.'* The farmer was equally cold stating *'then I shall farm no more'*.

In early spring Oswestry Council signed an agreement with the military authorities granting them use of the Horse Market and recreation ground as training grounds. One councillor asked what would happen when a circus visited the town. *'We get £10 from them for the use of the recreation ground,'* he said, *'are we protected for that?'*

'I think we can do without a circus now we have the war on,' the mayor commented. *'It is our duty to provide facilities for the training of these men.'* Back came the councillor, *'but we have a duty to look after the finances of the borough as well.'* The subject was left for the mayor and the town clerk to resolve.

By the end of April a solution must have been found for advertisements appeared stating that Pat Collins' Pleasure Fair would shortly be arriving for the May Fair, setting up on the recreation ground with shows, shooting galleries and new and novel attractions. A popular occasion, it brought scores of country people bent on both business and pleasure into Oswestry providing trade for local businesses.

An elderly Belgian refugee found drunk in Bailey Street by PC Pearce made headlines in late spring. *'He lay on the pavement in a helpless state and I was obliged to lock him up for safety,'* explained the constable. At the Borough Police Court the defendant admitted the offence. *'I had a pint of beer and a glass of whisky, and it was the whisky's fault,'* he declared, saying he was a respectable man with three daughters all engaged in munitions making. After expressing regret and promising not to touch whisky again he was discharged with a caution.

Transport passing through the town was an issue as June approached. Traffic had greatly increased since the arrival of Park Hall and some of the town's awkward corners were becoming very congested particularly near the station. Each evening, cars, carts and other vehicles passed each other in what was described as a bewildering fashion reminiscent of *'a sort of miniature Piccadilly Circus or Trafalgar Square'*. It was decided that a police constable be put on point duty during the busiest hours of the day before a serious mishap occurred.

Motor vehicles were not the only hazard; a runaway team of horses pulling a wagon made a bid for freedom in Oswald Street heading for the Cambrian railway goods yard, luckily soldiers in the area successfully stopped the runaways from injuring children who'd been playing in the road, by seizing the reins and pulling the team to a standstill.

Not all were appreciative of the force's help, however, an

Church Street, Oswestry. Probably a market day, note the pig to the left of the two men looking into the camera.

'Oswestrian' wished to know why two lady friends of his had been accosted by military policemen and told to get onto the footpath whilst walking down Church Street at 8.30pm. Further down the same street an order was given to two boys who were walking in the roadway. 'It would be interesting to know what authority the military police have over the civilian population of this town. Are we living in England or in Germany,' was the question asked.

Messrs R. and R. Hughes, Drapers and Outfitters, The Cross were in trouble with the law at the end of May 1916, charged with committing a breach of the lighting regulations introduced countrywide when bombing from the air became more likely by allowing a bright light to shine from their premises. The defendant pleaded guilty stating it had been left on by accident but was nevertheless fined 10s.

Lord Kitchener, whose death had so shocked Britain, was remembered by the Mayor of Oswestry at a meeting in the Guildhall. *'We can ill-afford to lose such a brilliant military leader and administrator,'* he said, *'a man who in the incredibly short period of two years has raised and equipped an army of 5,000,000.'*

On 13 June, heralded by a muffled peal of bells at St Oswald's Parish Church, a mid-day memorial service was held attended by the

A memorial card issued in memory of Lord Kitchener.

mayor, dignitaries and military representatives, including one man from each unit at Park Hall Camp. The service finished with the Last Post sounded by trumpets and drums followed by the National Anthem.

With the arrival of June problems with manning on farms were worsening. At a meeting of the Oswestry Agricultural War Committee one member who'd lost yet more workers despite an appeal, was moved to demand strongly, *'What is the use of this humbugging committee, when the military authorities do just what they like? What is the use of me coming here in these circumstances?'*

The chairman replied that he did not think they could do much to reverse an appeal, each case being dealt with on its merits; he would however, recommend that in future an Agricultural Committee member attend local tribunals.

In late June, with hundreds of extra customers from Park Hall attending the town's Post Office each week, arrangements for coping with them was being questioned in a letter to the *Advertizer.*

> *'I rejoice in our gallant lads,'* the writer starts off, *'I rejoice in the way in which townspeople endeavour to cater for their requirements. But in the hope that some powerful voice will take up the matter, I must point out that the scenes outside the Post Office nearly every night are a disgrace to the responsible authorities.*
>
> *These good men, after a day's hard work, come up town for a little relaxation and to post home letters. I see them nearly every night herded by the military police in a long line like animals going into the ark, save that they are all of one sex, with the result that time is wasted. Posts are missed, and everybody is grumbling, all because of the lack of foresight on the part of the post office people.'*

He ends with a plea for the Postmaster to *'do something'* as soon as possible. Action was swift, within a few weeks the town clerk received a letter from the Postmaster General informing him that problems in Oswestry would cease as shortly postal facilities would be provided on the grounds of Park Hall Camp.

With warmer weather at the end of June 1916 there were plenty of activities taking place in Oswestry to tempt both townspeople and those

The bandstand in Cae Glas Park, Oswestry, scene of many a concert.

from the outlying boroughs. A *'Lover of Music'* put pen to paper praising the introduction of weekly regimental bands performing in the bandstand in Cae Glas Park.

'The music played is some of the best and most of the bands have a richness of tone and effect which Oswestrians have rarely had the opportunity of listening to at home,' he states enthusiastically. *'Are the bandsmen being remunerated fairly? If not I hope the Town Council will make some effort to look a bit further than their noses in this respect. The present prosperity of the town is due to that Camp. Let us bear this in mind.'*

'Wanted' columns in the local newspaper were reflecting a change in attitude, actively seeking women to undertake what had previously been considered men's work. An advert placed by the Midlands Gas

Company was looking for *'one or two suitable girls of fair education to Learn Gas Meter Inspecting and Collecting, must not be under 18 years of age,'* a situation which would not even have been considered prior to the war.

At a July tribunal Parry and Jones, Tanners, appealed to retain two young male workers after older replacements hadn't come forward and found a novel excuse for not using women. When asked why they couldn't be hired as they were quite as careful as men with machinery and if they were suitably dressed there should be no danger, Mr Parry firmly explained, *'they have to stand on one leg at the shaving machine, and women can't do that, I'd be quite willing to take women on if they could do the work, but they can't and that's that.'*

In agriculture however women were finally being accepted. Female volunteers arriving in summer from Birmingham University where they had been training as teachers were joined by the wife of a Park Hall major to work on land in the Oswestry area. For their hard work the ladies were paid 1s a row for hoeing turnips, 3d per 100 yards for hoeing mangolds, and 1s an acre for cutting back thistles and hay gathering. It's interesting to note that a man would have earned 5s a day for cutting thistles, the farmers' point of view obviously being that it took two unskilled women to equal one expert man. The *Advertizer* on 26 July printed photographs of these ladies dressed in gym slips and shady hats, all earnestly wielding their hoes.

With so many soldiers billeted nearby, discontent was beginning to creep in with reports of general drunkenness and theft and men and women threatened in the streets. It was however, by no means one-sided; a local railway employee was taken to court in July charged with obstructing a sergeant major from the Military Garrison Police who'd been attempting to arrest a soldier. From evidence given at the trial it was obvious that military police were increasingly coming under attack from certain sections of the populace who would sneer, jeer at and insult them. On this occasion, the sergeant major surrounded by a hostile mob, had been head-butted in the face by the accused. In the general melee which followed, the man escaped but was re-captured shortly afterwards, he was sentenced to three months hard labour under DORA regulations.

On 7 August Garrison Sports day took place in the grounds of the grammar school, admission 6d, men in uniform free. The events were familiar, long jump, sack race, high jump, putting the shot, hurdle and flat races, tug of war, spar fighting, relay and obstacle races. Only the bomb throwing, bayonet versus bayonet, and officers' races gave any indication there was a war on.

Twenty-one injured soldiers in the care of the local Red Cross Hospital were given a treat midyear when a group of VADs arranged a trip for them on the nearby Shropshire Union Canal. Taken aboard a narrowboat, the boatwoman dressed traditionally for the occasion and the boatman in his Sunday best, they cruised the tranquil waters to Ellesmere, a small market town renowned for its meres. Tea was provided, cigarettes handed out, and a gramophone played, a pleasant memory to be treasured by those who would shortly be back at the front.

With labour becoming more difficult to source at the busiest time of the farming year, soldiers were taken on temporarily to help. Snide comments questioning their intelligence were made during a meeting of farmers with one reporting that when he had asked them to 'brush the hedges' (meaning to tidy up the twiggy parts left after the hedge

The canal in Ellesmere today where in 1916 recuperating soldiers were taken on a boat trip before returning to the front. (Bob Johnstone)

had been attended to with a brushing hook) they had done so using a broom. This caused much hilarity but angered one man who defended the soldiers' actions. *'How can a man from a non-agricultural background understand the term,'* he asked, going on to say that it showed the soldiers in a good light, they would no doubt carry out any order without question.

By now shortages of foodstuffs and other necessities were having an effect on shops in the town with limited supplies available. Lines of people waiting their turn had been irritated when *'temporary ladies from the Camp'*, as they were cuttingly referred to, were served before locals who'd been waiting some time. Traders were asked to remember that a time would come when 'this floating population' would be gone and old customers would not forget where they had received scant attention and little courtesy.

In September pupils at Oswestry Council Infants' school undertook to 'adopt' Private J. Alford of the KSLI, a prisoner of war recuperating at Interlaken in Switzerland after breaking his thigh. A letter soon arrived for the children giving them details of his situation.

> *'We are quite all right here at present staying at an English lady's house, called the Manor Farm, fifteen all told. It is something different to what we have been used to in Germany. When we got across the border into Switzerland, the people gave us a great reception. They threw us fruit, flowers, cigarettes, chocolate, and other things too numerous to mention. I was exchanged because of my leg; it is about two inches shorter than the other, and I feel confident they will fix me up all right here. I hope the teachers and scholars will accept my heartfelt thanks for their great kindness in adopting me.'*

In November grievances about young men exempted from the army riding around on motorcycles and in cars with *'apparently, very little else to do'* were being aired. A letter commented, *'if they could do this, then they should be in the army so freeing up married men with families and business responsibilities that were equally important for duty at home. Complaints are heard everywhere, about these joy rides, it is the duty of the police or somebody to acquaint the Tribunals and the military authorities of their actions.'*

And with Christmas Day approaching, twelve additional patients brought in to recuperate from their wounds at Ardmillan Auxiliary Hospital were just in time to receive from the Oswestry Women's Liberal Association a gift of fifty cigarettes and a box of matches each.

Whitchurch in 1916
At the beginning of 1916 readers of the *Herald* were able to understand what soldiers were experiencing when the paper printed an account sent by a Whitchurch soldier of his first night in the trenches:

> *'The only thing we have heard are a few stray bullets whistling by, but we are quick to learn the realities of warfare, we have been detected and are greeted by a storm of whizz-bangs* [a light shell] *singing over our heads. There is a terrific explosion, "By jove that was a near shave," says our guide. Next moment we make a dash for safety. "The dirty dogs," says an officer who has been out here for months, "they might have left you alone for the first time." And we entirely agreed with him.'*

Musical events were a popular way to raise funds throughout the war and towards the end of January a concert held in the Whitchurch Institute with various regimental bands performing and a selection of songs by soloists entertained both soldiers and civilians. A humorous number entitled 'Bob down, you're spotted' went down well with the audience.

The new compulsory and confusing Lighting Orders introduced early February under DORA led to one enterprising supplier in Whitchurch, Anthony Smith & Williams, Coach Works, quickly announcing that they were in the position to supply any of the equipment their customers might need to comply with the law. Sadly his advertisement appeared too late to help those up before the Bench in January when Whitchurch Petty Sessions had fined more and more Prees Heath personnel for riding motor cycles without lights.

The Lighting Order Regulations required everyone to make sure there were no lights showing from their homes and premises and with its introduction this ruling had led to a brisk demand for blinds and curtains in the town, a demand which retailers were not able to meet.

Local people nervously watched the skies no doubt praying that enemy aircraft would not appear as they waited for their orders to be supplied. A walk round the streets of Whitchurch as darkness fell revealed that not all were making an attempt to obscure light escaping from their windows. Workshops and even public buildings were still brightly lit with light flooding out over the darkened streets. For some reason, it was generally thought that windows to the rear of a property in the town did not need to be covered and this situation did not improve as time went by with more and more people becoming lackadaisical. A concerned householder hit on one solution, writing to the *Herald* to suggest that windows be covered over with brown paint or paper until proper blinds could be fitted.

Edward German, composer. Born in Whitchurch he often returned to his home town. (Ogden's Cigarettes Card)

At the end of March, townsfolk were pleased to learn that the composer Edward German, who had been born in Whitchurch on 17 February 1862, was paying a fortnight's visit to stay with his brother at The Laurels. A contemporary of Edward Elgar and Rudyard Kipling with whom he collaborated to write several musical pieces, he had trained at the Royal Academy of Music and was well-known as the composer of the operas 'Merrie England' and 'Tom Jones'.

A less than sympathetic account in the press in April reported on a traffic accident involving two motor cars and a motor cyclist in the Dodington area of Whitchurch. *'The motor cyclist's head damaged one of the lamps quite badly, but strange to say his injuries were not severe,'* the report states, ending by observing that because of the high speeds and amount of traffic in the area it was a wonder accidents were not more frequent.

In spring came a warning that carrier pigeons used for naval and military purposes had been shot in the vicinity as they headed for their

The Dodington area, Whitchurch.

lofts. Anyone found shooting the birds in the future would either be imprisoned for six months or incur a fine of £100 under Regulation 21a of DORA. *'Anyone not knowing the difference between doves, carrier pigeons and wood pigeons should refrain from firing at any birds,'* was the advice, *'and if any bird is found in an exhausted state it should be taken immediately to a police station or the military as it could be carrying very important information.'*

On 21 May 1916 British Summer Time came into operation. It was by no means a smooth transition in Whitchurch despite the parish church clock being advanced one hour at two o'clock in the morning to assist townsfolk changing their timepieces. A couple who had both advanced their clock one hour without informing each other awoke to a very early day indeed. Passengers on the Cambrian mail train from Crewe found that although they had boarded it at 1.20pm to travel the thirteen miles, by the time they arrived at their destination clocks were reading 3.20pm. Some individuals turned up for work one hour too early and had to wait for the gates to open to admit them, whilst parishioners attending one church arrived just as the service ended.

Probably most affected in all areas were the farmers who by tradition had always advanced their clocks one hour to ensure early rising. *'Cows and pigs don't like it,'* one local farmer commented, *'it is taking undue liberty with the life habits of self-respecting animals.'* It was the opinion at the time that the scheme may remain for some time; no one then could have foreseen it lasting indefinitely.

Animals were in the minds of supporters in June with money being raised for sick and injured horses abroad. The band of the 17th Cheshires played in various locations around the town whilst ladies sold badges in aid of the cause. With the Grand Picture Theatre also arranging benefit performances it was hoped to raise a considerable sum.

A quirky problem raised its head once again when the council's decision, taken earlier in the year, to close the swings in Jubilee Park on Sundays to both soldiers and the general public was discussed in a meeting. *'At least it provides soldiers with healthy recreation and keeps them out of mischief,'* commented one councillor. The resolution to re-open was carried by five votes to four despite strong opposition from the Reverend W. Hall who protested that such entertainment should not take place on Sundays.

Weekly tribunals were continuing to be heard with some exemptions allowed although increasingly these were only for a limited period. A market gardener, seventy-one years of age, appealed for his son, saying he was the only man left on his smallholding from where he supplied Prees Heath Camp with vegetables. An exemption of just three months was granted after which a medical examination would decide the son's fate.

August saw Whitchurch farmers, traders and locals gathering together to support the British Farmers' Red Cross Fund, which throughout the war raised many thousands of pounds through agricultural auctions. The funds obtained were used to provide motor ambulances, lorries and cars overseas as well as supporting British Farmers' Hospitals in France, Belgium and Serbia. Entertainment was provided in the form of military displays by soldiers from Prees Heath and the nearby Bettisfield Camp with a large crowd attending and enjoying the sunny weather. It was hoped to top the sum of £800, a figure well into the thousands in today's money, which had been raised on a previous occasion.

A scarcity of motor fuel was beginning to make itself felt in mid-August with groups who should have arrived in town to entertain civilians and troops alike unable to do so. Ladies, who up until the shortage had helped out at YMCA huts at the camp, found themselves unable to get there although some did manage to find alternative means. The *Herald* commented on the general discontent with the situation stating that it was one of the problems experienced due to the war and although very unfortunate this was no time for grumbling.

In September a fundraising concert held in the Town Hall by Queen Mary's Needlework Guild was hugely popular with some people having to be turned away from the door, probably due to the fact that the Duchess of Teck and her daughter Mary, who regularly stayed at nearby Ash Grange, were attending. A credible sum of £45 was collected for various causes.

A garden fete held at Prees Hall arranged by the local sewing party was taking advantage of the unusually mild weather in September, raising funds for wounded soldiers. The band of the 17th Cheshires from the camp provided music for both entertainment and dancing and a big attraction was the current clog dancing champion, Private Brennan, holder of both the Scotland and World Champion Belts who had agreed to perform. It was later reported that the event had been a resounding success increasing funds substantially.

Correspondence to the *Herald* in October 1916 was reflecting the very real fears many in the town had of being bombed by Zeppelins. The writer, who signed himself 'Common Sense', asks:

> *'It ill becomes any of us to show fear of death, when our boys are bravely facing it every day but this is confessedly a disagreeable form of exit, bombed from the starlit sky. Advice is needed, should we remain outside or go indoors to a sitting room or the cellar, although the latter course does not seem very plucky! Bedrooms on upper floors are probably more dangerous, really some advice would be welcomed by many.'*

He finishes by questioning why brilliant lights were still showing to the rear of numerous houses whilst other windows were darkened, a problem in the town which obviously hadn't improved from earlier in the year.

In October Whitchurch Traders' Association informed the public that closing times from October 1916 to March 1917 in Whitchurch would soon be brought in line with the rest of the country. The association appealed to the public to do their shopping well before dusk as, owing to lighting restrictions, it would be dangerous for people to be out on the darkened streets.

As the year approached its end, several local taxi and car owners took it upon themselves to arrange trips to surrounding towns for wounded soldiers from Broughall Auxiliary Hospital – with cigarettes provided. The idea, proposed by Mr F. Peel, was quickly taken up and it was hoped further trips would take place to brighten the lives of those who had suffered in the service of their country.

In mid-November and with food difficult to source, the *Herald*, anxious to help, was publishing useful recipes. Marrow jam and fried bread with cheese were two suggestions, although the ingredients for vanilla cream, *'one teacup of soaked tapioca to which add a pint of new milk, boil with a knob of butter, add two egg yolks and more butter and beat for ten minutes, top with beaten egg white, two ounces of sugar and a teaspoonful of vanilla'* must have been difficult to source for some.

Local stores were advertising Christmas treats for men currently overseas, with the Talbot Café in Watergate Street stocking Christmas plum puddings at 3s and 4s 6d each. *'Send Out to Your Boy at the Front!'* their advertisement urgently advises. Toys and dolls for children, and Christmas cards and presents to suit all could also be had at A.J. Crosse based in the High Street, although for some with their men away it would be a struggle to raise the Christmas spirit not to mention the money to afford such items.

The film 'Battle of the Somme' reached the Grand Picture Theatre in Whitchurch at the end of November 1916. Lloyd George, Secretary of State, had commented when it was first released, *'Be up and doing! See that this picture, which is in itself an epic of self-sacrifice and gallantry, reaches everyone. Herald the deeds of our brave men to the ends of the earth. This is your duty.'* Whitchurch responded to his plea for the film played to packed houses throughout the time it was available in the town.

And as the end of the year approached Whitchurch Rural District Council was discussing female labour. A letter sent to them by the Local Government Board had given details of how other local authorities were using women in various occupations, work which had

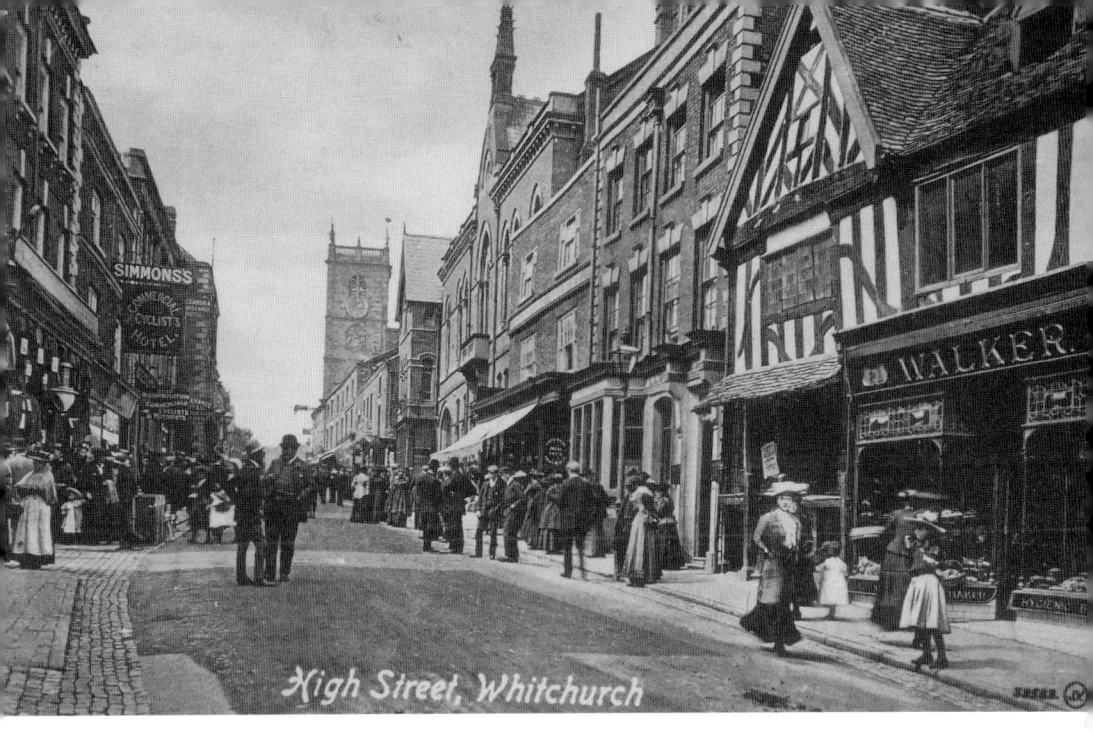

A busy shopping day in the High Street, Whitchurch.

generally been done by men. The clerk however, commented he did not see that such issues affected them at present and the subject was deferred.

With 1917 on the horizon the year drew to an end with the horror of the Battle of the Somme uppermost in everyone's mind. Thousands of men had now lost their lives in a war which still showed no signs of ending, whilst thousands more were being urged to sign up to replace them. The introduction of conscription meant fewer men were winning their cases for exemption at the tribunals and there were very real hardships at home with shortages of money, fuel and food. Along with the rest of Britain, many in Oswestry and Whitchurch must have wondered despairingly just how much longer the war would drag on. Those left on the home front longed for peace and a return to normality, but for the moment it was a case of carrying on as best they could whilst waiting with trepidation for news of their loved ones.

CHAPTER 7

1917
The War Intensifies

On 19 January 1917 a huge TNT explosion ripped through Silvertown munitions plant in West Ham, Essex destroying the factory and surrounding area and leaving sixty-nine dead and 400 injured. The year had started with depressing news.

Prime Minister David Lloyd George's newly-formed coalition government introduced the third and largest War Loan late January 1917, an action seen by some as tantamount to robbery. By the end of February the substantial amount of some £7,000,000 had been invested, mainly by small subscribers. Chancellor of the Exchequer, Mr Bonar Law was pleased to announce that Germany, who had commented sarcastically that figures would provide an indication of the real state of the country's financial strength, would now know that Britain's assets were still healthy.

With powers introduced under DORA over 2.5 million acres of land would be taken over by the Government in 1917 with War Agricultural Committees formed in each county. This ensured that, with most of the men who'd worked the land now overseas, together with the War Office's intention to take even more recruits off the farms, those left behind were suitably organised to produce adequate food to feed the country.

Lord Devonport, Government Food Controller, was sending out advice in February suggesting that the public restrict their eating habits, seeking in particular to minimise the amount of bread, meat and sugar being consumed. It wasn't until the end of the year that it became necessary to introduce compulsory rationing.

In early February theatres were screening the film 'The Battle of the Ancre', the final British attack with tanks in action that took place at the Somme in 1916 before winter arrived. Described as the most inspiring war picture the world had ever seen, it featured footage of men under fire in a sea of mud, tanks rolling across devastated landscapes and, away from the scene of battle, Tommies queuing up for mail, eating their rations and chatting with German prisoners. It brought home starkly to audiences the horror that was taking place abroad, drawing record crowds wherever it was shown.

Women were still, incredibly, resisted as replacements for men at the front by some farmers. This is obvious from the continued appeals at tribunals for exemption of farm labourers or sons, the reason cited being unable to get workers. Those in favour of women on the land however, supported them wholeheartedly, with proper training and a good record in care of stock and use of machinery, they were considered perfectly able to cope. Only ploughing was in some cases, still considered men's work with one farmer stating he would be very sorry to see a lady follow the plough.

By March 1917 Lloyd George was warning Britain that food stocks were alarmingly low. *'It is essential for the safety of the Nation, for the maintenance of the Nation, for the life of the Nation, that we should put forth immediately every effort to increase production for this year's harvest and the next,'* he urged adding there was also a need for more workers in woodlands and ship-building. *'Germany is wavering – let the men of England move against the enemy en masse, enrol for National Service today and back up the men in the trenches.'*

On 6 April 1917, President Woodrow Wilson went before Congress to call for a declaration of war on Germany by the USA. Germany's flouting of its undertaking to suspend submarine warfare in the North Atlantic and the Mediterranean as well as its attempts to get Mexico to join them against America resulted in the appeal winning immediate support from the Senate, although many Americans wanted to remain neutral. Eventually some two million US soldiers would go on to fight in France under Major General John J. Pershing.

At six o'clock on the evening of 25 May 1917, German Gotha heavy bombers attacked Folkestone resulting in seventy-nine deaths and leaving over ninety-six injured. The news spread rapidly, a new weapon had entered the arsenal of war with devastating consequences. In mid June the East End of London came under attack with resultant loss of life and property; one bomb struck a train entering a station, another dropped on a school. In all, 104 died and over 400 were injured despite retaliation by anti-aircraft guns. Following on from the bombers came German Zeppelins attacking an east coast town before being brought down in flames by a Royal Flying Corps pilot not long afterwards. With the increase in German aggression and the urgent need for retaliation by Britain, the Ministry of Munitions was calling for more workers. Many young women and girls responded, the work, although dangerous, offered good prospects and included maintenance allowance whilst training.

A significant piece of news spread countrywide on 19 June 1917 when it was announced that, due to anti-German feeling, the King and the rest of his family had renounced the family name of Saxe-Coburg-Gotha and from henceforth would be known by the title Windsor.

With autumn approaching a plea went out to schools for children to assist in harvesting horse chestnuts. These were to replace grain currently used in the production of acetone, essential as a shell propellant. Every ton of chestnuts gathered also meant half a ton of grain was saved for human consumption.

Soon it would be Christmas and people at home were once again sending off parcels to their loved ones, not knowing if they would ever receive their gifts. Another year and still the war marched relentlessly on.

Oswestry in 1917

The New Year of 1917 dawned wet and cold in Oswestry with few on the streets to welcome it, once again the weather and lack of street lighting discouraged many people from venturing outdoors. At the King's Theatre, a pantomime sought to raise the spirits. 'Cinderella' attracted large audiences, including men from Park Hall Camp. Soldiers of Scottish regiments had been delighted to hear an extra verse added to a song sung by Glad Eye, an ugly sister. *'Wait and see, wait and see, A change in camp football there's likely to be, When the Welshmen have found how more goals may be missed, The "Kilties" will climb to the top of the list, If you only wait and see.'*

Women working the land were now a common sight, gone were skirts and 'make-do', in came gabardine plus-fours worn with thick woollen socks, boots, shirt and tie, knee-length coat and broad-brimmed hat. Oswestry stores were quick to stock the outfits marketing them as *'suitable articles for Gardening, Farming, Motor Driving, and all outdoor occupations, each Garment being Fully cut to allow for the Freedom which is so essential to all Women Workers.'*

Newspaper reports now confirmed that women were quite able to cope with their men away. On a fifty-acre farm a farmer's two daughters cut all the hay, one driving the machine the other sharpening knives, a workman's wife single-handedly cut back twenty-seven acres of thistles, whilst a young girl managed the same task on eighty acres.

As shortages became more apparent local stores were doing their best to help their customers. Beckitt's Stores, The Cross were promoting dried fruit salad at 7½d a pound, *'Delicious and economical and saves sugar'*, it advised before suggesting the use of glucose which they could supply in any quantity for jam making.

W. Bradley and Company, drapers, warned their customers that the price of linen and wool would soon be prohibitive with cotton materials

Shopping at the Cross, Oswestry.

particularly costly. *'Buy soon, raw cotton is nearly three times the price it was a little over two years back, if you add to this the cost of dyeing materials, finishing and bleaching, and the difficulty in obtaining supplies and the shortage of labour...'*

Cambrian Railways advised that it was the ideal time to extend the egg and poultry trade with leaflets on raising chickens provided free of charge from their headquarters. This suggestion might have been prompted by news that in January alone Britain had imported over seven million eggs from Egypt and 360,000 from America.

In March Mrs Campbell of Oswestry War Agricultural Committee, encouraged any woman with time on her hands to take up the offer of five weeks free training on farms. A waterproof and a pair of boots would be provided if necessary and only those who *'did not think they were on a picnic and were ready to work long and hard'* should volunteer. If their parents were willing, schoolboys over ten years of age could also be put to work growing potatoes and vegetables and working no more than two hours a day.

Late in May 1917, the Shropshire Board of Education was urging every school to grow more vegetables. To its credit Oswestry High School for Boys was already producing food from allotments unlike the Boys' Secondary School. Here Oswestry Town Council's attempt at acquiring land for allotments had fallen on deaf ears, school governors suggesting that instead of school grounds, Cae Glas Park, the bowling green or the tennis courts be ploughed up. Firmly informed that the ground was unsuitable for food production, compulsory powers were applied for by the Town Council.

Mr G.G. Higham, Gun Maker and Sports Outfitter in Bailey Street, was offering a new innovation to those with families in danger advising them to *'Save the lives of your Relatives and Friends at the front by buying for them a "Light Steel Protective Waistcoat" which can be worn without any discomfort under the Tunic. Used extensively and with splendid results by Officers and Men in the British and French Armies.'*

The problem of lice – reportedly at least ninety-seven per cent of men in the trenches were infested – led to one local chemist advising the use of Harrison's Nursery Pomade. *'Kill That Insect, Tommy, Send your Pals "out yonder" some tins a little of which will kill every insect on hair or body, reasonably priced at 4½d and 9d.'*

With food stocks running low throughout the country and bread, meat and sugar rationed, one lady was shocked when a friend, asked if she would cut down on food had told her, *'we have never lived extravagantly so can't make any change.'*

'News of the daily toll of ships being sunk obviously makes no difference to some who can "keep a good table" and who are continuing to stick to their old routines, leading to others going short,' the lady said in a letter to the paper. *'It rests with the women to play the game, if they provide the same amount of food as always you can't blame their families for eating it.'*

> I CANNOT SEND YOU BANKNOTES,
> I CANNOT SEND YOU GOLD,
> BUT THIS SUGAR AND POTATO
> ARE MORE THAN WEALTH UNTOLD.

A postcard indicates the value placed on sugar and potatoes as stocks ran low in 1917.

With devastating losses taking place abroad grieving families were increasingly having to visit local outfitters Bradley & Co who offered costumes, coats, blouses, dresses, black trimmed millinery, black gloves, hat and arm bands, mourning handkerchiefs and veils for both women and children. It can only be imagined the great relief felt on receipt of a pre-printed postcard from abroad informing them that their

> NOTHING is to be written on this side except the date and signature of the sender. Sentences not required may be erased. If anything else is added the post card will be destroyed.
>
> [Postage must be prepaid on any letter or post card addressed to the sender of this card.]
>
> ~~I am quite well.~~
>
> ~~I have been admitted into hospital~~
>
> { ~~sick~~ } and am going on well.
> { ~~wounded~~ } ~~and hope to be discharged soon.~~
>
> ~~I am being sent down to the base.~~
>
> I have received your { ~~letter dated~~ _____
> { ~~telegram ",~~ _____
> { ~~parcel ",~~ _____
>
> Letter follows at first opportunity.
>
> ~~I have received no letter from you~~
> { ~~lately.~~
> { ~~for a long time.~~
>
> Signature only } Bert
>
> Date 25-7-17.

A pre-printed card completed and returned by a Shropshire soldier confirms to his relieved family he is still alive and well. (Bob Johnstone)

loved one was *'quite well and a letter would follow at the first opportunity'*.

At the beginning of March 1917 soldier labour was again offered to farmers and landowners on application to the Salop War Agricultural Committee. Agreement had also been reached by the authorities that all farm labourers necessary for the production of food could work on Sundays for the duration of the war. This decision did not meet with the approval of some and the Archbishop of Canterbury's support for the scheme was particularly welcomed. Asked for his opinion, he'd said, *'I have no hesitation in saying that in the need which these weeks present, men and women may with a clear conscience do field work on Sundays.'*

In April 1917 one local was prompted to write to the press expressing concern at the large numbers of people coming into town on market days then staying to eat and drink afterwards. He pointed out: *'These people have food at home and would be better off eating there leaving what was available for those who haven't the luxury. If they went home at midday after the markets had finished they would also be able to do some useful work on the land instead of becoming incapable of such through staying in the town,'* a veiled comment concerning drunkenness no doubt.

At the end of April 1917 a Food Economy Campaign was advising on the best methods of stretching food rations. Held by the National Union of Women Workers at Church House, cooked foods made with barley flour, maize and rice by the girls of the High School were on display, one much admired dish being potted beans, a substitute for potted meat.

With restrictions on sugar Oswestry war brides were no doubt relieved to see an advertisement by Morris's Café in nearby Shrewsbury offering wedding cakes made to Government regulations. Instead of icing, the cakes were covered with white satin and silver decorations and could be had for 10s 6d and upwards.

The May Fair was eagerly anticipated. Once again Pat Collins's Fair would be on the recreation ground, this time offering a Dragon Scenic Railway, Giant Steam yachts, lion show and electric Galloping and Walking Horses – a little light relief for soldiers and civilians alike from the trauma of war.

Tribunals with appeals for exemptions for a variety of reasons continued. An ambulance driver home from the front suffering from nervous debility, fits and loss of memory was asked if he had looked for work at local farms. *'Yes,'* was his reply, *'but the farmers said they did not want men,'* a comment met with laughter in the court, but little sympathy from those who judged, the applicant being firmly told he must find work at once and *'put his back into it'*.

In Oswestry news that a train carrying German prisoners would shortly be passing through the Cambrian Railway Station resulted in crowds gathering on the platform. The prisoners were being moved from a Welsh camp to undertake timber felling in the Kerry Forest, and were described as typically German, very fit and apparently pleased to be so far removed from the fighting line.

In June Oswestry War Guild were seeking ladies willing to help in a Hospital Work Depot with a meeting held at the Guildhall. Lady Harlech, in her opening speech, pointed out that judging by the numbers present who had answered the call, an excellent spirit to help existed in Oswestry. Later in the month a Red Cross Depot was opened in rooms above Parr's Bank, Church Street to make swabs, pads and pneumonia jackets for the sick.

Oswestry War Pensions Committee found itself dealing with increasing requests for allowances and grants from dependants of soldiers on active service. One case sited a wife who before the war had received 21s per week but now had to make do with 14s 6d per week separation allowance and 5s from a lodger. With two children and suffering from muscular rheumatism, she hired a woman for some

Cambrian Railway Station, Oswestry as it is today. (Bob Johnstone)

Brogyntyn Hall, home of Lord Harlech, in its heyday.

of her household duties and with 4s per week rent to pay felt she needed more money to survive. One member of the committee observed that as she hadn't her husband to keep, the family were better off than they were before the war. Another, a tad more sympathetic, commented that the applicant was certainly in a bad way. Back came the brusque answer, *'I suppose she was bad before her husband went away?'* Her appeal was turned down.

One woman describing hardship due to having two sons away fighting fared better and was granted 4s per week. *'Could not the second son allow his mother more out of his pay,'* the tribunal secretary had queried. *'Soldiers only get 1s a day, and when some of it has to be used to pay the French and Belgians for a drink of water there is not much left to send home,'* came the reply.

Two exciting events occupied the minds of local people in mid June 1917, both involving bi-planes, with one landing in the grounds of Brogyntyn Hall, owned by Lord and Lady Harlech, the pilot having lost his bearings and come down to ask his way. Later in the week yet another plane descended, this time to pick up petrol before the pilot's flight continued.

On August Bank Holiday Oswestry held a Sports Day on the cricket field, Victoria Road, entry 1s, men in khaki half price. As well as the usual athletic events, attractions included tug of war, boxing, wrestling, bicycle races and a baby show (prizes donated by Virol Ltd, Glaxo and

Nestlés) which, it was reported, was attended by over-heated mothers and babies, the latter protesting vigorously against the proceedings. Other games included an officer's race, one mile walking match and a comic singing competition, the singer required to hold a live pig beneath his arm whilst performing. That must have been worth seeing! The day ended with dancing.

Local people were perturbed to learn at the end of August that a prisoner of war internment camp was likely to be built at Park Hall to cope with the large number of German prisoners now in Britain. The Town Council immediately protested, aware that the close proximity of a PoW camp would cause much anxiety in the town; to no avail, however, as shortly afterwards the Royal Engineers arrived to begin its construction.

The issue of enough coal for the coming winter was worrying some despite an assurance from the Town Council that sufficient would be available, with one coal merchant assuring its customers they would be able to meet requirements. Nine other suppliers however, were not so sure and this news resulted in a flurry of letters to the press voicing concerns.

With tea increasingly in short supply, Beckitt's Stores was urging its customers to try coffee which was cheaper and more plentiful and could be supplied in the berry or ground. Cocoa was also advertised, its selling point being that it could be made with condensed milk thus saving sugar and milk.

Oswestarians were probably gratified to learn that an extra sixty-five street lamps would be lit over the coming winter months, doubling the number of the previous year. A petulant request to the Borough Surveyor's department that kerbs and steps be made more visible by whitening them however, received no reply. *'One can only suppose,'* opines a letter writer to the press, *'that our municipal "mandarins" do not go out after dark or it would have been ordered long ago. The life and limbs of us ordinary ratepayers apparently, do not count.'*

His comments must have been noted for by the end of October it was announced that seventy-six lights would be lit each night, assurance given to the residents that in the event of an air raid, they could be swiftly extinguished.

The Lighting Order was a continuing problem for traders in the town, one shopkeeper complaining of a drop in takings despite an 'open' sign being displayed.

'It seems absurd that at this distance from the East Coast, where several hours' notice of Zeppelins might be received, legitimate trade should be crippled by so unnecessary a precaution. What prospect is there of an enemy aeroplane coming all this way at the cost of gallons of petrol and enormous personal risk, to drop a bomb on Oswestry?

Even if there was a threatened raid by Gothas (German heavy bombers) *we should have plenty of time to prepare to take cover and put out lights. Is there a competent Military Authority or a Chief Constable who could see their way to relaxing these irritating, superfluous regulations.'*

The proprietor of the Queen's Hotel faced charges for allowing bright lights to shine from his windows on two instances in October 1917; his offence was considered serious as on the second occasion, police had received an air raid warning. He blamed a servant for the oversight and was fined £1 10s, plus costs for the special constable who had been on duty.

In mid October the Cinema Palace in Coney Green, Oswestry was showing 'The German Retreat and the Battle of Arras'. Most importantly for the Oswestry audience was the sight of the KSLI, together with the King's Liverpool Regiment, advancing in attack formation. The film showed in graphic detail the devastation inflicted on French villages, scenes from the battle, tanks in action, prisoners being taken and the wounded cared for. The Arras offensive, involving British, Canadian, South African, New Zealand, Newfoundland and Australian troops, ended on 16 May 1917, by which time over 160,000 Allied and 125,000 German troops had lost their lives.

A welcome reduction in bread costs, a four pound loaf now priced at 9d made little difference to Oswestry bakers' sales. One trader said that with such a low price he would now find it necessary to charge for paper to wrap the loaf in, although his customers could, of course, bring their own paper.

With Christmas 1917 approaching, Oswestry tradesmen were once again discussing trading hours. A decision to commence earlier closing from January through to March 1918, at 7pm instead of 8pm weekdays and 8pm instead of 9pm on Saturdays did not suit all. The mayor, chairing the meeting, took the opportunity to comment wearily that

KSLI silk Territorial Badge and a 'sweetheart brooch'. Made from a cap badge, brooches were sent home from the front to be worn proudly by wives and girlfriends.

some people were apt to *'forget there was a war on as this move would also provide traders with a greater opportunity to educate the public to shop early'*.

A report addressed to farmers and food producers from the Salop War Agricultural Executive Committee painted a chilling picture, not only of the current situation, but also of the future:

'If we are to secure food for the people of this country, greater and more prolonged efforts are required. We are threatened with shortage of food throughout the world, and not in 1918 only, but in 1919 and 1920. If we do not provide food for ourselves, no other country can or will, and to what extent we shall be short

of food depends upon the extent of our success or failure in increasing home grown supplies.'

Members of the Women's Army Auxiliary Corps (WAAC) passed through Oswestry on their way to Park Hall Camp to undertake clerical duties at the end of November 1917. They were thought to look very smart in their khaki uniforms although *'their feminine curls fluttering from beneath their slouch hats'* still, according to some, seemed out of place. Women had some way to go before they would be accepted as soldiers.

In October a plea that Christmas parcels for troops in France be posted before 1 December, failure to do so meant parcels would not reach their destination, resulted in a rush to comply. Shops were advertising suitable gifts. SEND OUR GALLANT SOLDIERS AND SAILORS A GIFT FROM BLIGHTY was one headline promoting mufflers, socks, helmets, gloves and 'hussifs' as suitable items.

And in mid-December the pantomime Robinson Crusoe starring Miss Yvonne Lamor as Crusoe and Mr J.P. Marsdon as Will Atkins 'the famous Winkapops', was drawing in audiences at the King's Theatre, Oswestry, another opportunity for people to forget their troubles.

Whitchurch in 1917

New Year 1917 was a relatively subdued affair in Whitchurch with many staying at home rather than taking to the streets. Newspaper reports had done nothing to lift the spirits, informing readers of a raft of further regulations which would shortly be introduced. These included the need for locals to register with local traders and obtain a ration card in order to obtain essential grocery items.

With food very much in mind in January 1917 the Cambrian Railway Company offered Whitchurch residents a chance to rent plots of land adjoining the railway for growing garden produce. With every inch of spare land needed and notices in newspapers continually warning of food shortages, these were quickly taken up.

Farmers were pleased to learn, in a special notice from the Agricultural Committee printed in the *Herald*, that shortly it was hoped to secure two motor tractors to assist in the ploughing of their land, something which was probably read with relief as many were having to manage with a drastically reduced labour force.

The threat of aerial bombing was now very real and residents in the town were aware of the need to obtain black-out material to prevent any light showing from their windows. A social held in St John's vestry, specifically to raise funds for the purchase of material, attracted soldiers as well as local people all glad of an evening's entertainment.

Whitchurch Petty Sessions judged an offence against the Lighting Order in February with a local man charged with driving a motor van without the headlights properly obscured or sidelights visible. The defendant protested that he had been teaching another man to drive and they had expected to get home before dark. *'I did my best to arrange the lamps,'* he informed the court, *'but the lamp burnt the paper on the disc so that it shone brightly, there was no danger of an accident.'* Nevertheless, he was ordered to pay costs.

In March the people of Whitchurch learnt that Edward German, native of the town, had composed music to accompany a song entitled *All Friends round the Wrekin*, lyrics by W.H. Scott, a journalist. The piece, a tribute to the county where he was born and its famous landmark expressed the friendly and patriotic spirit of Salopians, not only in peacetime, but also in their devotion to the nation and empire whenever needed

Whitchurch ladies had the chance to join a three-month gardening course from the local Agricultural Committee at the end of March. They would need to bring their own tools, an advertisement informed, and pupils would leave with full knowledge of how to manage production of crops. Lessons in poultry keeping and dairy skills were also offered and it was hoped many would participate. Particularly needed were women to learn skills in cheese and butter making, a large part of Whitchurch's trade. The ladies, on reaching the end of the course, would replace men now overseas and qualify as dairymaids.

Whitchurch Co-operative Society took out an advertisement informing customers of imminent new food regulations at the beginning of March advising that bread would be reduced to 9d per four pound loaf, sold for cash only and no dividend. They'd also managed to obtain, for the benefit of their customers, a large consignment of ladies and children's boots and shoes at prices which they said couldn't be repeated.

Protests on the outcome of recent tribunals were still causing problems with more and more decisions made by the military authorities called into question. One farmer, appealing for his son, reported that the boy had been called up three times and twice sent home as not wanted. *'We cannot carry on our work unless this harassing procedure is stopped,'* the farmer stated vehemently. At least twenty cases presented by a number of local tradesmen were granted exemption but were warned that this time short exemptions would be granted for the final time.

In April conscription was beginning to create a real shortage of labour in the town with Ernest S. Pugh, hairdresser and tobacconist, using the *Herald* to thank customers for past support and hoping that they would continue to support him now that many of his staff had been called up for military service. At the same time, local banks announced a reduction in their opening hours, again due to the numbers of staff, now serving in the military. Barclays, Lloyds, the Manchester & Liverpool District Bank (later the National Westminster), and the National Provincial would all now operate shorter hours opening from 10am to 3pm weekdays and 9.30am to 12 noon on Saturdays.

A concerned letter writer to the *Herald* was questioning the Urban District Council's decision to allow grazing of horses in Whitchurch's Jubilee Park:

> *'It must not be forgotten that the area was bought with public subscription for the specific use as a park, a place of recreation for children and young people and a place of restfulness for others. Let us increase its beauty not despoil it. Who would desire to attend a concert in a park strewn with horse dung, no, it is wrong to spoil our park this way.'*

By the end of the month local farmers were taking advantage of the motor tractors offered earlier in the year. The Titan, a sturdy American-built machine started on petrol before switching to paraffin to continue its work. Under the control of the Whitchurch War Agricultural Committee it was in great demand.

In May organisers of a Shower Day to be held in the Town Hall by the Whitchurch Branch of Queen Mary's Needlework Guild were seeking contributions to replace shortages of items for both troops at home and hospitals abroad. Having heard that Her Majesty had promised to accept gifts for distribution, one small child appeared with

Jubilee Park, Whitchurch.

her donation expecting to see the Queen ready to accept it personally; thankfully she was not too disappointed when she found out Her Majesty was in London. A thank you letter received from Queen Mary later in June praised the great efforts Whitchurch people had made on behalf of the Guild.

In May 1917 shortages of foodstuffs was leading to higher prices particularly eggs. A scarcity of potatoes, due to abnormally bad weather the previous summer and autumn, was also a problem particularly as the vegetable was often added to or even replaced flour.

At the beginning of June a meeting was held in the Drill Hall aimed at older men or those working in a reserved occupation, the purpose being to explain how they could join the Shropshire Volunteer Regiment. Well attended, it was presided over by Mr G. Baker, Chairman of the Urban District Council. *'The importance of a volunteer force to defend our homeland in the event of an invasion was invaluable,'* he explained, *'and the Government, under the new Volunteer Act, have promised provision of new weapons and ammunition.'* He finished by explaining that, for the duration of the war, attendance would be required on at least ten occasions and his enthusiasm for the cause resulted in twenty-six men signing up for service.

Local bakers and confectioners in Whitchurch were puzzled by the numerous and contradictory restrictions under DORA which had affected them. It was permissible for bakers to provide penny fruit pies with lids, although open tarts were not allowed, sweet buns were perfectly acceptable whilst meat pies were not. Many must have sighed deeply and carried on regardless.

Whit Sunday in 1917 was warm and showery but it didn't put off holidaymakers arriving in the town for a short break. Many made the journey to Prees Heath Camp to attend a sports day being held there, it was also an opportunity to admire the small gardens planted next to the huts created by a succession of soldiers as they passed through the camp on their way to war.

Despite being confined to his bed at Prees Heath Camp hospital, Private S. Hawke still retained his sense of humour sending in a story to the *Herald* which was considered amusing enough to print. Entitled 'Rough on the Buns' it tells of two Tommies in a railway refreshment bar. *'Puzzles me why these things are called Bath Buns,'* queries the first Tommy. *'Does it? Easy enough,'* replies his companion, *'It's because they're hard enough to scrub yourself with!'* A fact, confirms Private Hawke, who evidently had experience of railway fare.

A soldier recently moved from Prees Heath contacted the *Herald* concerning the appalling weather he had experienced since arriving at a coastal camp. *'On Tuesday we had a terrific storm and about midnight I woke from my dreams to hear the boys from a tent lower down singing at the top of their voices, "Throw out the life-line". Their tent had been blown down and they were saturated, but still cheerful.'* This latter remark reflected the stoic attitude of the soldiers who accepted all situations with humour.

In May a court case concerning disturbing literature distributed by three women pacifists to soldiers in and around Prees Heath Camp on 23 April made countrywide news. The women, two from Manchester and the third from Whitchurch, had been handing out pamphlets, originally printed in the *National Labour Press* and the *Daily News*, detailing the number of deaths so far in the war. Arrested and charged under DORA, at their trial the court heard that men who had been handed the literature, distributed from a donkey cart driven to the camp by Mrs Skinner, were given it with the comment *'we don't want all our young men killed yet'*.

After hearing the evidence of a number of soldiers, one of whom stated he did not expect to see such leaflets when he came home from the war, it was the opinion of the court that they had been circulated to cause disruption among the troops. The outcome of the trial was a three-month sentence for Mrs Skinner, her companion receiving one month, whilst the local woman was fined £2.

A report on the newly formed Volunteer Detachment appeared in the press at the beginning of July when Colonel Cholmondeley, commander of the 2nd Battalion Shropshire Volunteer Regiment, inspected a parade in the Smithfield. Adverse comments made previously about volunteers in Whitchurch were now thoroughly vindicated by their presence, Colonel Cholmondeley had told them, before going on to say that the country was by no means safe from a raid by the enemy and having a trained force such as those before him meant the success of the enemy was greatly reduced.

Concerns with shortages of foodstuffs from earlier in the year continued to be a problem in July 1917 with fruit now reported as particularly pricey. Requests being made for special sugar supplies for preserving, one method of providing food during winter months, received a decidedly mixed reaction too, some applicants obtaining their rations more or less immediately whilst others received no reply to their request.

As a result of the year's disastrous potato crop many local farmers were present at a talk from a representative of the Board of Agriculture on the subject of stopping potato blight by using Burgundy mixture, a mixture of copper sulphate and sodium carbonate. Anything that would improve output in the future was welcomed by those responsible for feeding the nation. Farmers also welcomed a break in the hot weather in July resulting in much-needed rain for their crops. With the harvest already in, those who had yet to gather theirs probably regretted missed opportunities as the rain continued indefinitely and fields became increasingly sodden.

Much praised at the end of July was the dramatic rescue of a child by Private Holding of the 76th Training Reserve Battalion at Prees Heath Camp. Private Holding, recently released from hospital and recuperating from injuries, on seeing a small child fall into the canal from the wharf in the centre of town, had immediately jumped into the water to perform a rescue. It was hoped he had not suffered further from the wetting he got.

In August 1917 Whitchurch town was canvassed on the subject of household and food economy. A meeting held in the Town Hall had not been well attended so it was decided that visits, together with leaflets on how to make economies, be made to all residents in the town. Later, in autumn, with the U-boat blockade tightening and posters reading *'save two thick slices every day and defeat the U-boat'* appearing throughout Britain, the message probably went home.

Aware that coal supplies would be rationed from 1 October 1917 by order of the Coal Controller, Whitchurch Salop Gas Company was advising that it had a limited number of modern stoves for disposal. *'A gas cooking or heating stove will lessen your anxieties this coming winter and incidentally aid the Ministry of Munitions to maintain an adequate supply of essential products for shells,'* it stated, hoping for a flood of buyers.

An accident in the High Street involving a motor engine drawing ten transport wagons and a hay trussing machine, under the control of soldiers, was causing excitement in October. The trussing wagon had run into the railings of the National Provincial Bank before demolishing a nearby front window. Fortunately, as it was dinner hour, the street was deserted and no one was injured.

Tribunals in Whitchurch were increasingly turning down appeals for exemption as the end of the year approached. One application by the military for the withdrawal of a certificate of exemption granted to the science master at the Grammar School was however denied, the reason given that the school would lose its grant if the subject was not taught.

In December restricted shop hours were introduced with businesses closing earlier, 6pm Monday to Thursday, 7pm Friday and 8pm Saturday, for the duration of the winter. Two signs, S.O.S. and S.O.B. spotted in one shop window were erroneously translated as 'sold out sorry' for butter and bacon and 'short of beer'. *'People will think there must be a war on somewhere,'* quipped one individual.

With Christmas approaching traders were advertising suitable gifts to send overseas, urging customers to buy soon. The Whitchurch branch of Queen Mary's Needlework Guild held a Christmas sale opened by Her Grace, Katherine, Duchess of Westminster. Many took advantage to buy their Christmas gifts, realising that the money would go to help their fighting men to endure the rigours of winter as well as helping the wounded.

So as 1917 drew to a close austerity was tightening its grip on those left at home, with panic buying having led to rationing of essential foodstuffs, coal and other items, now reluctantly accepted as part of daily life. By now over 260,000 women throughout Britain were employed in agriculture and men too old or not released to fight at the front had been formed into Volunteer Regiments to protect ports, main roads and railways should an invasion take place.

People at home were weary of war, growing increasingly dissatisfied with the life they had to lead and the constant worry concerning their families. It must have been with trepidation that those at home anticipated the new year of 1918; the thought very much in everyone's mind was just how much worse could the situation get and when would the boys come home?

CHAPTER 8

Oswestry and Whitchurch Heroes

From the onset of the First World War all over the country medals and awards were being presented to men who had distinguished themselves in battle and proved their bravery in many ways. Oswestry, Whitchurch and their surrounding districts were no exception winning recognition for local men which made the townsfolk who knew them very proud. The names of the towns' heroes who received rewards are far too numerous to list in entirety but there follows just a few of their stories.

***Croix de Guerre* (Cross of War)**
This was a French medal awarded to an individual or unit for acts of heroism involving combat with enemy forces. It was also awarded to foreign military allied to France.

Sergeant Alfred Thomas, a former employee of Mr Maclardy's Art Studio in Oswestry, was awarded the *Croix de Guerre* for distinguished conduct in the field during Eastern operations.

Distinguished Conduct Medal
The oldest British award for bravery, the Distinguished Conduct Medal was awarded in the field for gallantry by other ranks in the British and Dominion Armies.

Private Harvey Kynaston, Australian Imperial Forces, was a former native of Oswestry and employee of the Cambrian Railways, emigrating to Australia in 1911. He joined the Australian Imperial Forces in 1915 and took part in the fighting in the Dardanelles. He was awarded the Distinguished Conduct Medal by Lieutenant General Sir William Birdwood, commander of the Australian and New Zealand Forces, for actions taken during fierce fighting in France when he had served as a 'runner' of despatch messages.

Private J.H. Davies, Machine Gun Corps, who lived in Oswestry with his grandmother, also received the Distinguished Conduct Medal for gallantry in action. In September 1917 he had carried a wounded officer to a place of safety before returning to his post as a 'runner' carrying his messages through heavy barrage fire and delivering them at a particularly critical moment. Prior to the war he too had been an employee of the Cambrian Railway Works.

Gunner A. Morgan, Royal Field Artillery, born in Oswestry was awarded the Distinguished Conduct Medal having volunteered, together with two other men who subsequently died of their wounds, to keep two guns in action at a critical period when the battery was almost overwhelmed by heavy enemy fire. When the wires to the brigade headquarters were cut he volunteered to take a message through the enemy barrage. Successfully achieved, he returned with an answer to the amazement of his battery commander who had fully expected him to be killed. The medal was presented to him when he was on home leave by the Mayor of Oswestry.

Sergeant W.E. Kingstone, KSLI, of Albert Road, Oswestry one of the original Oswestry Pals had been employed by Messrs Morris and Jones, Glasgow House, Cross Street. He was awarded the Distinguished Conduct Medal for conspicuous gallantry and devotion to duty to add to the Military Medal he had already received. With British tanks out of action due to direct fire from an enemy field battery during an advance, and with the company stopped by machine gun fire, together with a party of nine men he attacked and captured thirty prisoners, killing the remainder of the garrison and opening up the advance to the whole company.

Distinguished Flying Cross
This was awarded for an act of valour, courage or devotion to duty whilst flying in active operations against the enemy to members of the

RAF and also formerly to officers of other Commonwealth countries.

Lieutenant N.E. Williams, RAF, youngest son of Oswestry Alderman C.E. Williams, received the Distinguished Flying Cross for gallantry in a bombing raid on an enemy aircraft station. He was interned in Denmark at the time of the announcement of his award having had to land in enemy territory due to an accident with his aircraft.

Distinguished Service Cross

This medal was awarded at the time of the First World War to officers of the British Armed Forces, Royal Fleet Auxiliary and British Merchant Navy and officers of Commonwealth countries.

Lieutenant R.B. Stewart, Royal Navy, born in Llanforda Isaf, Oswestry was on board HMS *Mounsey* in October 1918 and helped in the rescue of American soldiers who were en route to Glasgow and Liverpool on HMS *Otranto*. The *Otranto*, a former passenger liner, had been converted into a troopship and a collision with HMS *Kashmir* during a heavy storm resulted in *Otranto*'s sinking in Machir Bay, Isle of Islay. Lieutenant Stewart received the Distinguished Service Cross for playing a major part in the courageous rescue bid that resulted in hundreds of crewmen and soldiers being saved.

Distinguished Service Order

This military decoration was awarded for meritorious or distinguished service by officers of the armed forces during wartime, usually in combat.

Commander Alfred Edmund Godsal, fourth son of Major and Mrs Godsal, Iscoyd Park, Whitchurch and serving on HMS *Brilliant* in April 1918, was involved in the first Ostend blockships exercise to stop enemy U-boats getting out of the port. The ship came under a tremendous barrage of enemy fire from shore batteries and unfortunately the exercise was a failure; nevertheless it was reported that Commander Godsal's bearing and spirits had been very gallant. On 10 May 1918 another attempt was made to block the entry into the port of Ostend and again Commander Godsal was involved. This time the aim was to sink the ship HMS *Vindictive* in the channel, but again, despite these drastic measures U-boats still found a way through. It was during the resultant heavy fighting that Commander Godsal was killed by a shell; he is buried in Oostende New Communal Cemetery in Belgium.

Meritorious Service Medal
This was awarded for distinguished service or gallantry by non-commissioned officers.

Corporal T.B. Cartwright, Army Service Corps, formerly of Belton Road, Whitchurch had worked at the Whitchurch Herald prior to joining the army in November 1915. He was awarded the Meritorious Service Medal for valuable services rendered with the forces in France. He had also previously received the Belgian Croix de Guerre.

Military Cross
This was awarded to officers of the British Armed Forces and officers of the Dominions at the time of the First World War in recognition of an act or acts of exemplary gallantry during active operations against the enemy on land.

Captain Donald Nicholson, KSLI, of Park Issa, Oswestry was awarded the Military Cross for conspicuous gallantry and devotion to duty having led his company through heavy gas and highly explosive shrapnel shells. Further attacks by the enemy were also repulsed, the result being that Captain Nicholson was able to recover two Lewis guns and also lead men who had lost their officers across open ground under heavy machine-gun fire.

Lieutenant F.A. Bayley of 13 Church Street, Oswestry, who had been gassed at the Battle of Loos (which saw the first use of gas by the British) and wounded in the head by a shell was awarded the Military Cross for conspicuous gallantry and good leadership in an attack. His platoon captured eight machine guns with their crews together with other prisoners. He personally rushed one of the guns, killing two of the enemy and through his coolness and resource his platoon reached its final objective.

Second Lieutenant William Charles Beckett prior to emigrating to Canada had lived in Chester Avenue, Whitchurch and returned to Britain in 1915 as a private. In 1916 he received his commission and was attached to the KSLI. He was awarded the medal for carrying out a successful exercise and, despite being wounded at the start of the action, had remained with his platoon until the end.

Captain George Gordon Shone, Royal Field Artillery, of Woodhouses, Whitchurch also received the Military Cross in the New Year's Honours 1918, having been mentioned in despatches in 1917.

Second Lieutenant Paul Humphrey Clarke, Royal Garrison Artillery Special Reserve, of Ash Corner, Whitchurch was awarded the Military Cross for his heroic actions in battle.

Captain J.E. Young, Royal Army Veterinary Corps, a former veterinary surgeon based in Station Road, Whitchurch, was awarded the Military Cross in 1919 in recognition of his service on the Western Front where he had been in the thick of the fiercest engagements.

The Reverend R.W. Dugdale, Army Chaplain, was the second son of the Reverend Sydney Dugdale, Rector of Whitchurch; he received the Military Cross for having rendered valuable assistance to the wounded whilst under heavy shell fire without the slightest regard for personal safety. In 1918 at the age of twenty-nine he was killed by a German shell during a heavy barrage.

Military Medal
This was awarded for bravery in battle on land to members of the British Army and other services and at the time of the First World War to personnel of the Dominion countries below commissioned rank.

Gunner William Lloyd Maclaren Francis, eldest son of Mr T. Francis, a grocer in Beatrice Street, Oswestry, was awarded the Military Medal for coolness and skill during action at the Battle of Cambrai on 2 November 1917. On 20 November he also brought down a two-seater German aeroplane with his Lewis gun and went on to rescue the wounded under heavy shellfire.

Lance Corporal C. Williams, Machine Gun Corps, of Chemistry Road, Whitchurch, received the Military Medal for an act of great bravery during battle in March 1918. His actions were placed on record by Major General S. Lawford, who stated that Lance Corporal Williams had showed great gallantry and devotion to duty when the water used to cool down his gun and stop it jamming had boiled away. Despite being wounded he crawled through heavy fire, filled a tin with water, and brought it back to his gun after which he continued to fire on the enemy.

Corporal Llewellyn Passant, 1st Monmouthshire Regiment ,of Sherrymill Hill, Whitchurch, joined the Monmouthshire Regiment in

1914. He received the Military Medal in recognition of his bravery when in June 1917 under heavy fire he had assisted in bringing back wounded men, his courageous conduct and leadership were recognised and highly commended.

Victoria Cross
This is the highest military decoration awarded to members of the armed forces of any rank for valour in the face of the enemy.

Lieutenant Colonel John Vaughan Campbell OBE of the Coldstream Guards was a well-known figure in Oswestry living as he did with his family at Broom Hall on the outskirts of the town. He was to be particularly remembered for his actions at the Battle of the Somme at Ginchy, France in 1916, not only by the townsfolk of Oswestry but also countrywide. His exploits on that day were also thought to have inspired two cartoons published in Punch magazine at the time. One, entitled 'the dream' depicted a sleeping colonel dreaming of following the hounds, whilst the other entitled 'the reality' showed fighting men in the trenches.

Colonel Campbell was in command of the 3rd Battalion of the Coldstream Guards when on 15 September 1916, seeing his remaining men and officers taking cover in shell holes to escape from the enemy's fierce machine-gun fire, he quickly realised they were losing touch with each other. Colonel Campbell's adjutant and second in command had already been killed; only four officers were to survive that day, and the colonel knew that drastic action was required. Taking from his pocket his silver huntsman's horn, which he carried throughout the conflict, he sounded the 'tally-ho' indicating to his men that they should re-group. His men were well used to the sound; he had used the horn many times to rally them, its ringing tones being recognised more easily than the whistle used by other officers. Colonel Campbell was to say later that his 'men immediately came running in from the shell holes just like the hounds from the cover, they knew it was me'.

Re-established, the 3rd Battalion lined up and moved forward bayoneting the German machine gunners; this event was later recognised as one of the most deadly machine-gun attacks the Germans had set up on the Somme.

Having taken the trench and backed up by the Irish Guards, the Coldstreamers and Grenadiers continued pushing forward seeing before them the enemy clambering out of their trenches, dug-outs and shell holes and running away. Finding themselves stopped from pursuing due to barbed wire entanglements, the men cheered when tanks, recently introduced into battle by the British, appeared and quickly flattened the obstacles.

On 16 November 1916 Colonel Campbell was awarded the Victoria Cross by the King at Buckingham Palace and promoted to the rank of Brigadier General. On returning home to Oswestry the following day his car was stopped in Beatrice Street, Station Road and the Cross by the sheer number of people who had come out to cheer him. Responding to cries for a speech he said, 'Thank you, it was my lads that did it, to them is all the credit', before continuing his drive to Broom Hall. Oswestry people were heard to say that they hoped the good luck that had so far persisted, as Brigadier General Campbell had never been injured, would last until the end of the war and this proved to be the case. He was also the holder of the Distinguished Service Order received for actions taken during his time in the Boer War.

Private Harold Whitfield, KSLI, formerly of the Shropshire Yeomanry and son of an Oswestry publican, was awarded the Victoria Cross in May 1918. Whilst in action in the Battle of Tell 'Asur he had single-handedly charged and captured a Lewis gun, which had been harassing his company at close range, before disposing of the operators, turning the gun on the enemy and driving them back with heavy casualties.

Harold's aunt at Pool Farm was happy to pass on an extraordinary dream she had had a few nights before. 'Only the other night I dreamt that Harold had won the Victoria Cross and now it's true,' she told an *Advertizer* reporter.

Oswestry Town Council reacted quickly with arrangements made for a civic welcome when Harold next arrived home on leave. The presentation, an address in album form and £250 in War Bonds, took place in Cae Glas Park on 13 June 1918 with thousands present to witness it. A military band played and speeches were made by dignitaries including local MP Mr W.C. Bridgeman, now Parliamentary Secretary to the Ministry of Labour, Lord and Lady Harlech and the mayor. After the presentation Sergeant Whitfield thanked them and was loudly cheered when he said he had done his duty as any Englishman would. The event ended with a rousing chorus of God Save the King.

It wasn't until June 1918 that Harold Whitfield was presented with the Victoria Cross by King George V in Leeds, his heroic deeds read out to the large crowd by Lieutenant General Sir John Maxwell.

Wilfred Owen – Oswestry's War Poet
Wilfred Owen, a son of Oswestry destined to become world famous as one of the greatest of Britain's First World War poets was born on 18 March 1893 to Thomas and Susan Owen at Plas Wilmot, a large red-brick house built in the mid-1800s on the outskirts of the town.

The house belonged to Susan's father, Edward Salter, and on her marriage in 1891 to Thomas Owen who worked for the London and North Western and Great Western Railways, the newly married couple lived with the rest of the family at Plas Wilmot. Two years later Wilfred Edward Salter Owen was born beneath the high Georgian-style coved ceiling in the main bedroom.

By 1897, due to Susan's father's monetary situation, Plas Wilmot was in the process of being sold in order that debts incurred could be settled. For a short period Susan, Thomas and Wilfred moved to Shrewsbury to live with Thomas's parents whilst he sought work. It wasn't too long before Thomas was successful in his application for the post of station master at Woodside Station, Birkenhead, resulting in the family moving to the suburbs of Tranmere where Wilfred was to attend the Birkenhead Institute.

By 1910 the family had moved back to Shrewsbury, Thomas Owen now had a post at Shrewsbury Railway Station as Assistant Superintendent for the Western Railway region, and they were living in a three-storey house Mahim, in Monkmoor Road. Wilfred's education continued at the Shrewsbury Borough Technical College, adjacent to the town's English Bridge, working as a probationary teacher-pupil.

Reaching the age of eighteen Wilfred undertook a brief spell as a teacher-pupil at Wyle Cop School in Shrewsbury and during this time sat the University of London Scholarship examination; unfortunately he failed to make the grade. Whilst waiting to retake the entrance examination and prompted by his mother's fervent religious beliefs and his own thoughts that he might take up the priesthood, he became a lay assistant to Reverend Herbert Wiggin, vicar of Dunsden, a parish near Reading. Whilst there, in his spare time he attended the University College, Reading studying botany and poetry.

His experiences with the old, sick and impoverished whilst in Dunsden had a profound effect on Wilfred leading to a deeply felt disillusionment in the church and its practices. He hated to see the conditions the villagers lived in and felt there should have been more done to assist them. By February 1913, suffering from a mental and physical breakdown Wilfred had returned to Shrewsbury to recuperate.

Again unsuccessful when re-taking his university scholarship examination it was at this point that Wilfred left England, taking up a post at the Berlitz School, Bordeaux where he taught English for the next two years. Despite the outbreak of war in September 1914 it was another year before he volunteered for the army.

On 21 October 1915 Wilfred Owen enlisted in the Artists' Rifles Officers' Training Corps spending seven months at Hare Hall Camp, Essex. On 4 June 1916 he was commissioned as a second lieutenant, on probation, in the 2nd Manchester Regiment. Moving around different camps he found himself close to the town of his birth in October 1916 having been sent to Park Hall Camp, Oswestry. It is very likely that whilst at Park Hall he undertook the training of troops in rifle use on Caer Ogyrfan, the Iron Age hill fort on the northern outskirts of Oswestry where practice trenches had been dug to imitate those that would be found in France. The poem 'Storm' is also believed to have been written whilst he was at the camp.

In January 1917 Wilfred Owen and his men were seeing action on the Somme having been told to take control of two German dugouts filled with two to three feet of mud and water on the front line along the Serre road. For fifty hours they held out whilst the Germans kept up a constant bombardment, the blinding of one of his men is believed to have inspired his poem, 'The Sentry'. In a letter to his mother he wrote, *'I have suffered seventh hell. I have not been at the front. I have been in front of it. I held an advanced post, that is, a dugout in the middle of No Man's Land...'*

In March 1917 Wilfred was in hospital having received a mild brain injury after falling into a cellar. Just a few weeks later, on 14 April 1917, he was back with A Company, 2nd Manchesters who, together with the French, were taking part in the bitter fighting and coming under heavy artillery fire at St Quentin, northern France as they attempted to capture the Dancour trench from the Germans, a trench incidentally, that was found to be empty when reached. Wilfred Owens' poem 'Spring Offensive' is believed to relate to the horrific experiences he underwent during this time when, having been hit by a shell blast at Savy Wood, he lay with the horribly mutilated body of a friend until finally found.

Not long afterwards it was noted by the company medical officer that Wilfred was becoming more and more confused. Diagnosed with shell shock on 1 May 1917, he was transported to Craiglockhart War Hospital, Edinburgh to recuperate. Here his doctor, Dr Arthur J. Brock and Siegfried Sassoon, who was also recuperating and had become a friend, urged him to write his poems. The poems he produced at this time are thought to be some of his best work as he strived to expose the horrors of war although there were some who accused him of being a pacifist and a coward. It was during this time that Siegfried Sassoon introduced Wilfred to other writers, H.G. Wells, Robert Graves and Arnold Bennett.

By November Wilfred had been discharged and after a short break was posted to the Manchester Regiment's Reserve Battalion based in Scarborough. Letters sent home at this time revealed his decision to return to the front and in September 1918 he was back in the trenches in France having rejoined his regiment. During this time he proved those who had accused him of being a coward to be in the wrong, taking over from his company commander who had been wounded as the allies tried to break the Hindenburg Line at Joncourt in October 1918 and capturing an enemy machine gun in full view before using it to drive away the enemy. Between August 1917 and September 1918 Wilfred Owen produced some of his most emotional work with perhaps 'Dulce et Decorum Est' and 'Anthem for Doomed Youth' best known. All of his poems passionately revealed his hatred of war, the absolute futility of it, his pity for those who lost their lives, his admiration for the men who fought and his hate for those who sent men to their deaths.

Wilfred Owen was killed on 4 November 1918 during the crossing of the Sambre-Oise Canal, his unit having been ordered to 'cross the canal and engage the enemy, there is to be no retirement under any circumstances', he is buried at Ors Communal Cemetery in Northern France. The devastating news of his death, which happened just one week before the Armistice, was received by his mother on the very day she would have heard the bells ringing out to celebrate the end of the war.

On 30 July 1919 his family received the Military Cross in recognition of Wilfred's courage and leadership in 'inflicting considerable losses on the enemy'. The citation read:

> *'2nd Lt Wilfred Edward Salter Owen, 5th Bn. Manch. R., T.F., attd. 2nd Bn. For conspicuous gallantry and devotion to duty in the attack on the Fonsomme Line on October 1st/2nd, 1918. On the company commander becoming a casualty, he assumed command and showed fine leadership and resisted a heavy counter-attack. He personally manipulated a captured enemy machine gun from an isolated position and inflicted considerable losses on the enemy. Throughout he behaved most gallantly.'*

The majority of Wilfred Owen's poems were composed between August 1917 and September 1918 and at the time of his death just five of them had been published; it wasn't until later that he became well known. His ambition to show 'the pity of war', however, had been met in the compelling imagery his words painted in the many poems he left behind, words which are still as relevant today as they were in the era in which they were written.

A memorial erected to Wilfred Owen, English war poet born in Oswestry on 18 March 1893. (Bob Johnstone)

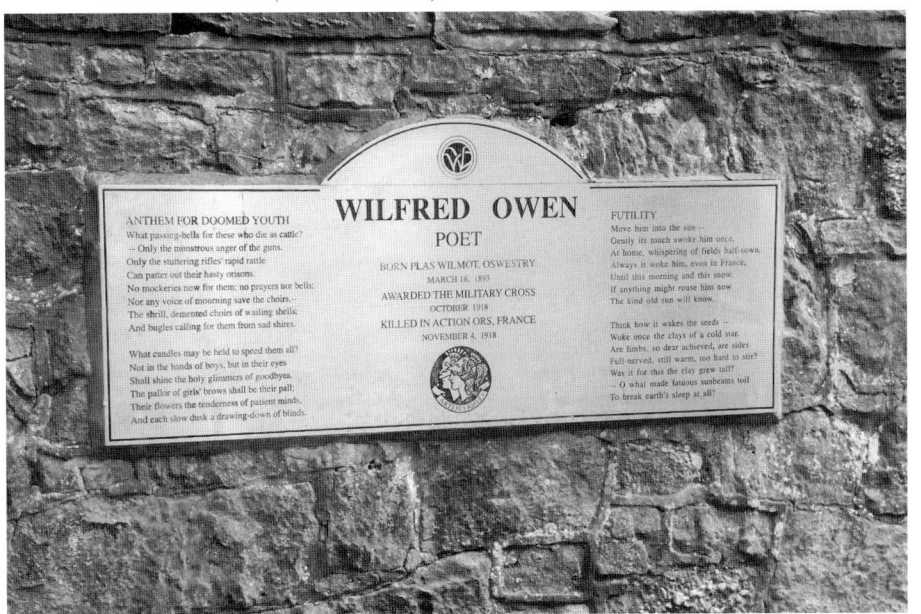

CHAPTER 9

1918
And so it ends...

❖

At the beginning of 1918, with food increasingly in short supply, there were real concerns of how Britain would manage in the coming year. London and the Home Counties had already seen meat and fat rationing introduced and in January 1918 the Ministry of Food introduced ration cards for all. Sugar, meat, margarine, butter and milk were now on the restricted foodstuffs list for everyone including King George V and Queen Mary.

At the beginning of April restrictions introduced meant hotels, restaurants and boarding-house owners could serve no hot meals after 9.30pm, with all lights having to be extinguished at the latest by 10pm until 5am the following day; theatres and dance halls were required to see lights out by 10.30pm. Despite newspapers publishing the facts, there were still some who remained ignorant of the new arrangements and were taken by surprise when asked to leave, probably in the dark!

News that Tsar Nicholas II had been assassinated by the Bolsheviks made headline news on 17 July and was received with horror throughout Britain. At first it was thought that Tsarina Alexandra and the rest of the family had been moved to a place of safety but this later proved incorrect; all of the royal family and their servants had been shot.

On 5 August the last Zeppelin raid on Britain was intercepted whilst crossing the North Sea in daylight. Five airships were involved and

King George V and Queen Mary.

one, L70 was brought down in flames by gunner Captain Robert Leckie flying in a Royal Air Force DH4 bi-plane piloted by Major Egbert Cadbury; his success ensured that the remaining four quickly returned to their base.

On 11 November 1918 at 5am, in a stationary railway carriage in the Forest of Compiègne, thirty-seven miles north of Paris, the signing of the Armistice between Germany and the Allies took place, signalling a prelude to negotiating peace. Hostilities should have stopped by 11am but it took another six hours before the fighting officially ceased. It was with elation that newspapers throughout Britain reported that the war was over with the Allies' terms accepted by Germany. The Kaiser immediately abdicated and the Crown Prince renounced the throne, leaving Socialist Friedrich Ebert to be elected as first President of Germany.

Negotiations would continue on into 1919 with seventy delegates representing the thirty-two allied and associated powers meeting together to draw up treaties at the Paris Peace Conference. It would not be until 28 June 1919 that the Treaty of Versailles, the Allies' formal peace treaty with Germany, was finally signed.

As Christmas approached the Prime Minister's wife, Margaret, sent out a personal message of greeting thanking women workers for the noble work they had done in helping the great cause of the Allies.

'Millions of men left their wonted tasks in offices, factory, forge and field to take part in the great fight for human freedom and simultaneously millions of women, many of them with frail bodies and unaccustomed to strenuous toil, came forward and cheerfully undertook all the work connected with vital industries of our land. Sisters one and all, I greet you this Christmas time, made so full of joy by the fact that the great conflict to which you so unselfishly set your hands, has now been brought to a speedy and victorious conclusion.'

Oswestry 1918
At the beginning of 1918, with the introduction of compulsory rationing, the Oswestry Food Economy Committee was appealing to the inhabitants of the borough:

'Study your ration and live within it. Avoid waste of any sort. It is useless for our brave sailors to risk their lives to bring us food if we waste it, the Food Controller is bringing down prices and securing equal distribution, do your bit. Save or starve.'

Following closely on this announcement the Chairman of the Food Economy Committee, W.H.C. Jemmet appealed to organisers of dances in the town not to provide food as part of the entertainment. *'Unnecessary consumption is in itself waste, whilst any profuse display of food conveys a false impression of plenty at a time when the most stringent economy should be practised.'*

Compulsory rationing did, however, please at least one person in Oswestry who pointed out that those like himself who were already eating voluntary rations would welcome it. *'About time too,'* he commented, *'those who ignore the appeals to patriotism should be made to do so, otherwise it means that some of us are cutting down our meals so that others may guzzle and gorge.'*

Lady Harlech went to the trouble of providing local housewives with a recipe for homemade bread utilising potatoes in the ingredients. With potatoes plentiful and their use encouraged as a replacement for wheat, this recipe must have been tested in many a kitchen. Later in the month a recipe for potato butter made its appearance, involving fourteen ounces of mashed potato blended with two ounces of butter or margarine and a small amount of yellow colouring.

Cooking courses held at the girls' high school kitchen were helping to eke out rations too with teacher, Miss Robson, demonstrating maize trifle, potato shortbread and maize and oatmeal biscuits, all of which did not use flour. What was produced, according to those who sampled it, was 'very nourishing'.

With rationing now a part of life, some 18,000 people from the town and outlying areas had registered with their preferred traders by mid-January, although the need to do so did not please all, resulting in frequent letters to the press. This led to the chairman of the Food Economy Committee, exasperated by the complaints, making an appeal that *'we abstain from grumbling and growling. It does no good and may do untold harm.'*

The introduction of meatless days on Wednesdays, Oswestry's market day when many were coming into the town for the livestock

A typically hectic day at the cattle market, Oswestry.

sales and needing to eat, led to market traders and local hostelries alike complaining to the Food Economy Committee that their trade would suffer, all to no avail as the ruling was upheld.

At the end of January, Mrs Finch-Jackson secretary of the Oswestry War Guild received a letter concerning three bags of socks sent out to the front for Christmas. Captain Shearer thanked the Guild writing:

'They are indeed most welcome and make a delightful Christmas present for the men. I had the pleasure yesterday, Christmas Eve, of handing them to my men, who are delighted with them. Please convey our most sincere thanks to your members. We are well and cheerful, I am thankful to say, and live in hopes of an early victory and the end of the war.'

The introduction of air raid precautions in Oswestry despite Shropshire's distance from the coast was the cause of much comment. The advice given was that in the event of an air raid, the bells of St Oswald's Parish Church would ring for three minutes; people were told not to congregate in crowds but rather stay indoors or take the nearest cover.

Street collections continued to be made almost weekly to raise money for hundreds of deserving causes and some were beginning to tire of continuously being asked for money. To promote a new way of giving the YMCA introduced Gift Week in aid of the military. Donations of whatever could be spared were welcomed, books, magazines, musical instruments, games, walking sticks even furniture. These were then distributed to soldiers at camps and hospitals at home and abroad. Particularly touching was the reaction of two children, a little girl who brought in three pencils and the offer of nine marbles from a small boy. *'Evidently children fully appreciate what the khaki boys are doing for us,'* was the comment.

With eggs still needed for hospitals, one man was complaining of the lack of organisation when pupils were sent out from schools without any method of recording their collection success. *'I and my neighbours are pestered with children who call, generally on their way home from school, to ask for eggs for Ardmilland 'Ospital, for the blind men, or for the 'Mind'*[sic] *sweepers,'* he complained demanding that some sort of order be imposed.

As the bitter winter weather and austerity measures continued, news that the annual Oswestry Fair would take place on 2 and 9 March 1918 with Pat Collins and his new and novel amusements once again attending, was welcomed enthusiastically, something to look forward to at least.

A Sergeant's Dance given by the 4th Reserve Battalion of the Royal Welsh Fusiliers in the Drill Hall, with music supplied by the regimental band, was another popular diversion and those attending were amused by the custom of 'eating the leek', an entertainment introduced by soldiers of Welsh Regiments stationed at Park Hall. It was reported, however, that persons who had partaken of the leek had great difficulty finding ladies to partner them afterwards in the dances.

After four years of war Oswestry shops and traders were still feeling the need to assure their customers that their goods were home produced. R.J. Fullwood purveyors of annatto, a kind of food colouring, and rennet, pointed out firmly in an advertisement that they were *'a British firm which has always been British. Germans have never had any interest in our firm which has been carried on by British partners using British capital since it was founded 133 years ago'*.

An Aeroplane Week held from 4 to 9 March saw Hobley's Tea

The Regimental Band of the Royal Welsh Fusiliers.

Rooms based in Church Street, Oswestry, advertising that *'the Government requires us to raise £25,000 for the cost of four aeroplanes, why not raise £50,000 sufficient for eight planes?'* A timely move, as one month later on 1 April 1918 the Royal Air Force and the Women's Royal Air Force was created from the Royal Flying Corps and the Royal Naval Air Service.

A report from the Oswestry War Agricultural Committee must have given farmers scant hope when it was announced that, despite sufficient horses available for ploughing, unfortunately the committee could not 'beg, borrow or steal more ploughs'. One change visible to all was the increasing use of tractors on farms. J. Gittens Ltd, Motor Engineers of Oswestry informed farmers they could take orders for a limited number of Fordson Tractors. *'One tractor replaces three or four horses on a farm and enormously extends the possibilities of agricultural production,'* their advertisement read. The price for a tractor, produced in a British factory, was £250 plus the delivery charge.

At the beginning of May Lady Harlech was concerned by the problem of wasps on soft fruit. She warned, *'We are threatened with a great plague of wasps, and with the importance of the fruit crop it is essential to kill all the queen wasps now.*' The method she recommended would not find approval today. *'I find it an excellent plan to offer a prize for the children in our schools who bring in the largest number of "corpses" to the schoolmaster, in one week I hear children have killed over two hundred,'* she wrote.

A suggestion that the Shropshire Union canal be used for passenger traffic was discussed in May 1918. Already utilised for Sunday School and choir outings, a proposal was put forward that it be used for a regular service. People living in villages and small towns with no railway connection would certainly have benefitted from the return of the fly boat which in earlier times had regularly travelled non-stop, day and night. The idea was only thought to be viable however, as long as passengers were not in a hurry to reach their destination!

Four seats for the wounded, given by Holy Trinity Soldiers' Institute were installed near to Cae Glas Park gates as summer approached. Before long someone observed that others as well as the wounded were using them. A scathing letter soon appeared in the press referring to the users as the 'sun corner men' who evidently found the seats a pleasant change from propping up nearby houses. *'Let seats be provided in the shade for these "weary willies"'*, suggests the writer, *'otherwise let them move on.'* The comments returned a quick reply lambasting the writer who had complained for his superior and ill-informed attitude and picking up on the fact that some of the men referred to knew what it was to be wounded or were elderly.

War Weapons Week with flags, bunting and posters appearing around the town took place in Oswestry from 15 to 20 July 1918. A suggestion that company advertisements in newspapers carry a plea to buy War Bonds was quickly taken up, one depicting a heavy gun in the hands of British Tommies. *'Fire your money at the Huns, join the patriotic investors who all this week have been hurrying to lend their money to the country, draw out your savings and buy War Bonds, back up our lads at the front with the full strength of your bank balance,'* it encouraged. A total of £7,000 was raised in the first two days rising by the end of the campaign to £55,437.

Oswestarians learnt that the town's Empire Theatre was to be dismantled and sent to France where it would be erected behind the lines to provide entertainment for the troops. German prisoners were used to move the heavy structures through the streets on its way to the railway station, causing much amusement for the locals as the Germans 'bore the burden of the Empire' upon their backs.

With the onset of autumn free food from the hedges became very important due to the failure of the 1918 fruit crop. Everyone was urged to go out into the fields and hedgerows to gather the fruit, with dealers offering to buy any quantity of blackberries. One Oswestry market trader advertised he would take at least one hundred tons of the fruit for which he would pay 3d a pound.

As agriculture became more and more mechanised towards the end of the war Crossley Oil Engines were advertising their product. Its advertisement read: *'Can be operated by any odd man about the farm, with only one cam and one lever, there is nothing to get out of order, can be used to cut chaff and slice roots, run pulping machines or operate saw benches.'* Many men returning after the war would find themselves replaced by a machine. As harvest time approached farmers learnt that for the cost of board, lodging and a small fee soldiers were available to help bring it in. One arrangement not working was the employment of German prisoners, one farmer reporting he had applied but been told there was insufficient manpower at the camp to provide an escort.

With winter once more on the horizon Bradley & Co, Drapers, not a store to miss a chance, was urging customers to come and see their one thousand pairs of woven combinations priced from 2s 6d to 17s 6d per pair, warning that with coal shortages in the offing warm underwear was going to be absolutely essential.

The use of Park Hall Camp to house prisoners of war was again under discussion by Oswestry Town Council. Councillors were not happy at the thought of it interning German prisoners, citing the lack of useful work available locally. As in the previous year an appeal to the War Office returned a prompt reply that temporary occupation of the camp by German prisoners was inevitable.

News that the Armistice had been signed arrived in Oswestry a little after 10am GMT on Monday 11 November, approximately the same time it reached Park Hall Camp, and was greeted with elation. Flags immediately appeared in the streets and on public buildings whilst businesses suspended activities for the day. St Oswald's Church bells rang out at regular intervals and in the evening exuberant crowds paraded late into the night with men, women and children filling the streets and waving flags.

The following day thanksgiving services were held at the many churches in the town, all of which were crowded to capacity and, with Christmas not far away, Bradley & Co were the first to take the opportunity, through their advertisement, of wishing regular customers their very best wishes for the first Christmas for four years under peace conditions.

The general election on 14 December 1918 was the next issue uppermost in people's minds as year end approached. It was the first election in which women over the age of thirty, occupiers of property or married to occupiers, and all men over the age of twenty-one, were allowed to vote. Mr T. Morris, Labour, stood for Oswestry, and a meeting of the Party at Powis Hall on 7 December particularly welcomed women. On election day however, although polling many votes he lost out to Conservative Viscount William Bridgman.

Meanwhile the commandant of Ardmillan Auxiliary Hospital, anxious to dispel rumours that the hospital was closing down before Christmas, let it be known that a convoy of wounded men from various battle fronts had reached the hospital on 20 December 1918. Due to the rumour, not many Christmas gifts had arrived for the wounded soldiers and she hoped that this situation would soon be rectified.

A letter received from a Shropshire Yeomanry soldier in Belgium spoke of the reception troops had received as they marched up a recently captured town street. *'In half an hour I had more kissing than I ever had in all my life,'* the soldier reported, *'old ones and young ones, pretty and otherwise, and all sorts of delicacies, cigs also champagne given to us.'*

And as the end of 1918 approached there was shocking news that Park Hall mansion in the grounds of the camp had been totally destroyed by fire at midnight on Boxing Day. Despite the best efforts of several fire engines, nothing could be done to save the old mansion but soldiers, probably from the Royal Inniskilling Fusiliers, earned great praise for helping to remove artefacts still in the mansion, as did German prisoners.

Whitchurch in 1918
In January 1918 officials at Whitchurch Cheese Fair reported that only six tons of cheese had been displayed, not a quarter of what was needed by the traders. *'It is an established fact that there is a shortage of*

An impressive array of cheeses on show at the Cheese Fair, Whitchurch.

cheese which cannot be attributed to farmers building up supplies,' the local newspaper said, *'farmers are sending as much milk to market as possible it being winter, no doubt in summer when milk yield is doubled, the situation will improve.'*

As increasing numbers of casualties continued to be brought into the area, Broughall Auxiliary Hospital supplementing its facilities by opening a new ward over the stables containing ten beds. *'If any of your readers can give or lend beds and bedding I should be most grateful,'* a letter to the press from the Commandant H.T. Lambert read.

The *Herald* was appealing to its readers in its editorial mid-January hoping that their customers would continue to support them as at the end of the month, owing to shortage of paper, its weekly paper would be reduced to five pages meaning that regrettably some of the usual features would have to be discontinued.

Love, the donkey, an animal put up for sale throughout the war by her owner Mr H.P. Gregory to raise funds for the British Red Cross was being auctioned again in early February at an event organised by Whitchurch and District Agricultural Society. A large proportion of the amount raised, £1,241 6s 8d, came from the sale of the animal.

Due to lighting restrictions a young lady was in court in February charged with riding a bicycle without lights. When taken to task by a Special Constable she had declared that it was a pity that he had nothing better to do. *'She did not show the respect for the majesty of the law that she should have done,'* the Special told the court who promptly fined her 7s 6d. Bike riders seemed to be a dangerous breed in Whitchurch, for in March the local post woman knocked down a man in Brownlow Street.

The arrival of hundreds of housewives from Crewe, first appearing on market days at the end of January equipped with large baskets to buy up supplies, was a continuing problem in Whitchurch, resulting in shortages particularly of meat, bacon, butter and margarine for the locals. *'Too many visitors from other towns would not be welcomed in the future,'* a councillor said. Tradesman were quickly served with a notice from the local Food Control Committee informing them that henceforth they should only serve persons who could produce their sugar cards.

In March 1918 news that local women Emily Stephings and Isabella Hardy had been taken on by the Shropshire Constabulary as women police officers met with great interest. They worked two shifts of four hours each, one particular task being to move on women who had taken to congregating near to Prees Heath Camp, a nationwide problem described as 'khaki fever'. The local police constable, described as a 'shining ornament' was warned he would have to look to his laurels. It wouldn't be until 1920 that Emily and Isabella at last finished their work.

By the end of March a communal kitchen set up by the Food Economy Committee in the Town Hall was seeing an average of 200 local children partaking of corned meat and potatoes, dumplings and boiled rice or vegetable soup, all of which, it was reported, was eaten with relish. For mothers who were trying to stretch out meagre rations, particularly as a notice to ration meat had just been announced by the Food Control Committee, this move must have been a godsend.

The headline ALL HANDS TO THE SPADE in the *Herald* brought to readers' attention the urgency of producing more food with the local district council appealing for land which could be used as allotments. Jubilee Park was mentioned but met with resistance from one councillor: *'There are gardeners and gardeners, allotments require good management and the Parks Committee would have something to say about untidy allotments in the Park. It would be better to see what the demand is before cutting up the Park.'* Maybe he'd never been hungry.

A welcome diversion in the form of Bronco Bill's great Wild West Exhibition and Mammoth Circus was taking place on Highgate Field in May with a depiction of life on the prairie performed by cowboys and girls, Indians and fiery mustangs. The spectacle of the attack on the Deadwood coach, two performances a day whatever the weather, proved a big draw with many attending to see this rarity.

A Great War Charities Fete and Flag Day was held during May Bank Holiday with military sports and horse jumping contests offering prizes of £5, £2 and £1. A greasy pig race and wounded men's sports were also included, together with a 'knock the hat off the Kaiser' shy. Dancing to the military band of the ASC took place in the evening, admission 1s, men in khaki 6d. *'To heal the wounded your help is needed,'* said posters advertising the event and Whitchurch responded admirably with an attendance of over 7,000 people. Money raised went to the Cottage Hospital, Broughall Auxiliary Hospital and various other good causes.

A jubilant report in the local press pointed out that despite U-boats, air raids, short rations, 'no beer notices', DORA, lighting restrictions, hard work and unfairness, people put on their holiday attire and smiled, smiled, smiled:

> *'What a people,'* declares the writer, *'and when local historians come to deal with Whitchurch and its part in the Great War in the future, a red letter day will be Whitchurch's Bank Holiday Monday 1918.'*

In mid May a special meeting in the Town Hall was advertised under the heading 30,000 WOMEN URGENTLY REQUIRED FOR THE LAND. Captain Sir Beville Stanier Bt, MP for Ludlow and Newport, together with other speakers gave speeches followed by a film of women working on the land. *'With the harvest approaching your help is desperately needed and as it is already known that women have done sterling work in assisting in the planting of approximately one million acres of potatoes I know Whitchurch will continue to do its bit.'*

Whitchurch Urban District Council was still debating the subject of aliens in and around the town in July 1918. *'This council protests against enemy aliens still at liberty, the time has arrived when all of them should be interned,'* declared one councillor. *'I should say the time had long since passed, it should have been done long ago, we have been four years at war,'* said another; the prior suggestion was passed unanimously.

In July the National Salvage Committee was asking Whitchurch Council to arrange for the collection of fruit stones and nutshells required for a special war purpose. It was decided to write to local schools asking children to collect all they could find. Although the reason was not released at the time it was revealed after the war that they had been needed in the production of carbon filters for gas masks.

At the end of August a report in the paper caused a flurry of comment. Independently two women had arrived in Whitchurch by train. Finding out they were going to see their husbands at Prees Heath Camp they decided to share a taxi cab. As they chatted they discovered that the man they were going to see was married to both of them! At the man's trial for bigamy the accused said he had left the first wife because of her temper and the second to save her life. One wonders how it all ended.

During War Weapons Week 12–17 August Whitchurch was doing its bit to raise money for aeroplanes, guns and ships. Local traders included the event in their newspaper advertisements urging 'Have your share in the triumph, Victory will be great' and 'Have your Money Ready.' An incredible total of £88,149 was raised by the people of Whitchurch and the surrounding districts, the highest total obtained in one week by any town in Shropshire apart from Shrewsbury.

Along with every other town in Britain, on Sunday, 10 November, Whitchurch was anxiously awaiting confirmation that an armistice with Germany was a possibility. The following day, with information that not long after eleven o'clock on the eleventh day of the eleventh month, a ceasefire had taken place people immediately crowded into the streets together with workers granted a holiday by their employers, celebrating the good news with elation.

It wasn't long before the streets of the town were decorated with flags and bunting with the banner of St George, the Stars and Stripes and the Red Ensign flying from the church tower. Once more, the chiming of the St Alkmund's Church clock could be heard ringing out over the town to the delight of small children many of whom had never heard it before. By the following day nearly every house in Whitchurch was displaying a flag and at night, lights shone out from houses and shops lighting up the streets, this despite retailers still being controlled under restrictions, due to the coal shortage, imposed by DORA which wasn't quite finished yet.

At last Whitchurch could anticipate a peaceful Christmas and soon local stores were advertising a range of gifts. Something to look forward to was a great Victory Ball to take place in the Town Hall on 1 January 1919. *'Get your "Allies" costumes ready and be sure to attend,'* read the handbill. Proceeds would be given for the benefit of the Wounded Soldiers' Fund at the Cottage and Broughall Auxiliary Hospitals.

The dispersement of soldiers from both Park Hall and Prees Heath Camps continued into 1919 and life began to return to normal in the streets and homes of Oswestry and Whitchurch. Forces men lucky enough to have survived found that after four years of war they were returning to a very different world to the one they'd left in 1914. A world in which political, economic and social problems would all raise their heads in the years to come and one in which there would be no going back to pre-war values.

CHAPTER 10

1919
The Aftermath...

❖

At the end of 1918 people in Britain had experienced their first old-fashioned Christmas and New Year for four years. A sprinkling of snow covering the ground on Christmas Day added to the festive feel and with the relaxation of some of the Food Controller's decrees traditional festive meals had been within reach. With the advent of 1919 people in towns and villages throughout Britain were looking forward to welcoming home their men, the lucky survivors. With nearly three quarters of a million British forces killed during the four years of war and more than a million and a half severely wounded, it was rare indeed if a family hadn't been affected; just fifty-two villages in later years earned the title of 'Thankful Villages' having lost no-one to the conflict. Men returning home to Britain and civilian life little realised that as they set foot in 'good old Blighty' they were carrying with them a deadly virus. The virus had found the trenches an ideal place in which to breed and men sent to field hospitals to recover both at home and abroad quickly infected others. Spanish Flu, so called because the first reported cases were in neutral Spain where there was no news blackout unlike many countries, was a particularly active strain that could kill in a day. It was first recorded in Britain at the beginning of the summer of 1918.

During the second week of July an outbreak of Spanish influenza made an appearance in Whitchurch. All elementary schools in the borough immediately closed until the following week to bring it under control and, although just one week later the schools re-opened, they had to close again immediately as even more cases occurred. By October there was little sign of the influenza abating, schools were closed in Oswestry and advertisements in newspapers were offering cures with Veno's 'Lightning Cough Mixture' claimed to be the world's supreme remedy for all manner of complaints including Spanish Flu. Bovril also took the opportunity to advise that their meat extract was an ideal pick-me-up for those who were recovering.

By November 1918 drastic measures to control the influenza outbreak were needed with Dr Beresford, medical officer for health, closing all schools and ordering that churches be disinfected and aired. Church parades were discouraged, cinemas put out of bounds for the military and places of entertainment sterilized between performances. It wasn't until the end of the month that there were signs of the epidemic ending.

At the beginning of November military authorities at Prees Heath swiftly put places of entertainment such as public houses, restaurants and meeting places out of bounds to try and stop the spread of the epidemic and by mid month it seemed the measures were working as the problem was abating.

But with Armistice Day celebrations taking place and men, women and children congregating in their thousands in the streets it had been easy for the disease to find victims. It seemed particularly cruel that some of those who'd survived the war were cut down just as peace was declared, equally cruel for their relatives who'd looked forward to life returning to normal thinking that soon their loved ones would be safe and sound in the bosom of the families.

The virus in Britain finally lessened towards the end of the year and by then, ill-equipped to deal with the epidemic, the country had lost a quarter of a million to the disease, with children even inventing a skipping rhyme – *'I had a little bird, its name was Enza, I opened the window, and in-flu-enza.'*

Female roles had changed drastically during the conflict and it had been proved over and over again what women were capable of achieving. With demobilisation however, the authorities were endeavouring to persuade women and girls to return to their pre-war jobs, mostly as domestic servants. Many flatly refused, having tasted a different way of living wishing to stay in the work they had been involved in over the previous four years. A great deal of ill-feeling developed as men sought to find employment; many thought that women should vacate the work they had come to enjoy in favour of men. It wasn't until the Sex Disqualification Removal Act, made law in December 1919 which also granted women the right to enter the professions, that it became illegal to exclude women from most jobs.

On 19 July Peace Day celebrations took place in London with 15,000 troops led by Allied commanders marching in a parade ending at a temporary plaster and wood Cenotaph designed by Edwin Lutyens and dedicated to the 'Glorious Dead'. Thousands lined the route and the day ended with a spectacular firework display in Hyde Park. A message to the wounded from King George V read:

'To these, who cannot take part in the festival of victory, I send our greetings and bid them good cheer, assuring them that the wounds and scars so honourable in themselves, inspire in the hearts of their fellow countrymen, the warmest feelings of gratitude and respect.'

Oswestry in 1919
Although the fighting had ceased on the Western Front at the end of 1918, fundraising continued with a grand whist drive and dance in aid of Ardmillan Auxiliary Hospital taking place at the Victoria Rooms on 9 January. Victory dances were also arranged in the Drill Hall with a band and a fancy dress competition enjoyed by a large audience.

With men returning home permanently injured or disabled, advertisements headed TRAINING FOR CIVILIAN EMPLOYMENT were appearing in the press advising that if men were no longer able to do their pre-war work due to their injuries, training as dental mechanics or watch and clock repairers was one area open to them. Another option was in the market garden trade with a local company at the beginning of March advertising suitable work for any disabled sailors and soldiers who contacted them.

As there was no longer a need for army horses or mules at the front, those that had been brought home were being offered for sale from camps and depots throughout the county, a chance for farmers and carters to purchase a good animal for a bargain price.

Victoria Rooms, Oswestry. An imposing building erected in 1864, it was used extensively for meetings during the war. Today it has been turned into apartments. (Bob Johnstone)

Belgian refugees were also returning to their homes. Their hosts, anxious to see them leave with happy memories, organised special events prior to their departure and many were sad to go, declaring that they would never forget the kindness they had received or the new friends they had made.

In Oswestry an item in the newspaper highlighting a proposal that, with the end of the war both the conditions and the wages of domestic servants in the future would need to be referred to the National Union of Working Women (NUWW), led to several letters. Many women and girls made it very clear that they had no intention of returning to domestic service with its 'yes mum' and 'no mum', and its tinkling bells at all hours, a particular complaint being that many servants were given a name such as Mary-Ann or Susan instead of being addressed by their real name. Those seeking servants would find it more and more difficult as time went by and women found alternative occupations.

Stories that Park Hall estate, now the army were vacating the grounds, had been bought by a well-known firm of soap makers for the purpose of erecting works and a garden city were doing the rounds early February. Major Wynne Corrie, when interviewed, said that it was the first he had heard of it and the rumours were dismissed as unfounded.

Oswestry Flower Show which had been cancelled during the war years was the subject of a meeting held in the Guildhall for all those interested in its revival and along the same lines, Oswestry Cricket Club called a meeting in the Memorial Hall to discuss resuming its programme of matches. *'For many years this club was one of the leading clubs in the area and it is hoped that the Cricket Club's efforts would be backed up by all lovers of sport as there must be many boys returning home and school leavers to carry on this fine old tradition,'* read a report.

Oswestry Council was holding yet more discussions on housing needs in February with three areas of land ear-marked for the erection of houses for the working classes. One councillor was against the proposal, he thought that one site would be enough, three an unnecessary expense.

The news that Mr Tims was leaving the area, retiring as organist and musical director from Holy Trinity Church, a role he had had for twenty-five years, led to a presentation of a cheque and silver salver being made. Together with his band, he had performed at countless functions put on to raise money for various causes throughout the war, as well as contributing greatly to keeping up the spirits in the town.

The Soldiers' Club, a haven for troops passing through Park Hall Camp during the war years and now disbanded, was holding an auction early February selling off caterer's cooking equipment, furniture, chairs, tables, curtains, and numerous other articles no longer required, no doubt a good place to pick up a bargain.

A report on Women and Public Activities in February prompted one lady to write to the local newspaper; it was her opinion that every parish council should include at least one *'broad-minded, loving-hearted mother, who would ginger up the dear, dull, prosaic fathers of the parish, whose chief business seemed to the keeping in order of footpaths.* When asked how a woman could be involved in such a role and look after her family, she replied, *'I should put the tea on the table before I went to the meeting and the master and bairns could help themselves, or go without till I came back as we do not possess a maid.'* This reply showed very clearly the changes in attitude which had occurred over the four years of war.

Traders who had been discussing ways of bringing their rural customers into the town by rail or road prompted one disgruntled woman to hit out. Having been told in the town to get her sugar 'in the country' during rationing, she felt that traders were now anxious to capture the trade recklessly thrown away when Park Hall had been active. *'I did get my sugar in the country and intend to do so in the future,'* she said firmly, *'no matter what nice joy rides they invent to get us to Oswestry.'*

St Oswald's Parish Church held a meeting mid-March to decide on the design of a memorial to local men who had fallen in the war. A sketch of the proposed monument drawn by architect George Gilbert Scott who had built the Albert Memorial, was on view for the congregation to approve. The memorial to the fallen of 1914-1918 was eventually erected in the church with money raised by public subscription.

Cae Glas Park gate pillars were also chosen to display the names of those who hadn't returned home with the names of the fallen, incised on marble plaques, put in place in 1921. In later years other names would be added, this time to those who had made the ultimate sacrifice

Memorial to the fallen erected in St Oswald's Church, Oswestry.

Cae Glas Park, Oswestry. After the war new gates were built as a memorial to Oswestry and district men who had lost their lives.

in the Second World War and in 2014, at a cost of £23,000, the gates were entirely restored having been badly affected by weather over the decades.

In January 1924 Cambrian Railway Company erected a memorial in Oswestry Railway Station in remembrance of the part their ex-employees had played in the conflict. Sculpted by A.G. Wyon in the form of a female figure, Honour, it was made of bronze and marble and listed the names of fifty-three Cambrian railwaymen who had lost their lives. With the closure of the line in 1966 the station building was sold to new owners and in 1975 the decision was taken by the council to have the memorial moved to Cae Glas Park where it was re-erected just beyond the main gates.

Whitchurch in 1919

As the New Year began life in Whitchurch was slowly returning to normal and already a more light-hearted feeling was beginning to make itself felt. A recent snowfall saw one hundred girls from Whitchurch

Memorial to Cambrian railway men who had died in the war. Unveiled in 1924 in the railway station, it was re-erected in Cae Glas Park in 1975 following the station's closure in 1966. (Bob Johnstone)

The road outside the boys' grammar school, Whitchurch. In 1919 it was the scene of an exuberant snowball fight between girls and boys celebrating the end of the war.

High School challenging fifty boys from the Grammar School to a forty-five minute snowball fight, the local newspaper gleefully reporting that despite the difference in numbers the boys were clear winners.

A Victory Ball held in the Town Hall early January drew a large crowd and was reported as a great success raising the sum of £25, the money being divided equally between Broughall Auxiliary Hospital and the Cottage Hospital, both of which still needed support.

At the end of January more and more familiar faces were seen back on the streets as men received their tickets and returned home. It was with pleasure that it was announced that members of the Whitchurch Police Division had now exchanged their khaki uniforms for blue and were resuming their duties within the town.

A memorial to the fallen in Whitchurch was under discussion early in the year, most favoured the suggestion that it take the form of a statue in stone or marble with the names of those who had fallen inscribed upon it. At first Jubilee Park was considered as a location,

The memorial opening ceremony at the junction of Station Road and Queen's Road, Whitchurch. (courtesy of Peter Lea)

Triptych form war memorial featuring a mosaic of St Michael in St Alkmund's Church, Whitchurch. Given by the parents of Lieutenant Thomas Chesters Bowler who died aged 19, it commemorated all Whitchurch men who had lost their lives. (Bob Johnstone)

but due to a spate of continuing vandalism with benches thrown into the canal and fences broken, this idea was abandoned. Eventually a memorial inscribed 'In proud and grateful memory of the men of this town who gave their lives in the Great War 1914-1918 "Faithful unto Death"', built in the form of a stone obelisk was erected at the junction of Station Road and Queen's Road.

Another memorial, this time in triptych form, the centre panel depicting a mosaic of St Michael, was placed in St Alkmund's Church. Dedicated to 'The Glory of God and in memory of the Whitchurch men who died in the Great War', it was given by the parents of Lieutenant Thomas Chesters Bowler who died on 3 October 1918 aged just nineteen.

Despite the war being over people in Whitchurch soon learnt that rationing was still in place with registration by customers still required. One exception made countrywide however, was the supplies of sugar for sweetening purposes in the buffets and canteens on railway stations and landing stages, this to enable the large number of men from His Majesty's Forces returning home to enjoy their first proper cup of tea for many a long year.

A meeting of the Whitchurch Agricultural Society held in February took the decision to defer their next show until 1920. The treasurer was, however, proud to announce that during the conflict the society had raised the substantial sum of £3,292 8s for the British Farmers' Red Cross Fund and would, in future, also undertake to support the Agricultural Relief of Allies Fund which had promised substantial donations to enable countries abroad to get back on their feet.

With men looking for work the local Employment Exchange was doing its very best to encourage employers to take on men who had come through the war. *'They risked their lives for you. Are you going to give them a job?'* read their advertisement. Any man who six months after applying had not found employment would have to join the dole queue and one outcome of the continuing situation of unemployment was the foundation of the British Legion in 1921 specifically to support ex-servicemen and their dependants.

At the beginning of February war work at Whitchurch Cottage Hospital was finally over and it was returned to a purely civilian facility. No fewer than 351 wounded men had passed through its doors during the conflict and a vote of thanks was proposed for the staff, medical officers and committee for the continuous service that had been rendered.

In March a sale took place at Broughall Auxiliary Hospital selling men's underwear, shirts, beds, mattresses, tables and household utensils. Yet another house which, having done its duty during the war, would shortly return to its previous state with all memories of the war obliterated from its rooms, corridors and outbuildings.

Life after the conflict...
At the beginning of 1919 women who had been widowed by the war resigned themselves to the fact that it was now up to them to cope as best they could without the support of their menfolk. From henceforth they would have to manage the home, control what money came in and make decisions on their families' behalf, a concept which four years previously would have been unthinkable, as generally it was the men who made all the decisions within the home.

'Pip, Squeak and Wilfred' medals awarded in 1920 to the lucky ones who returned home. (Bob Johnstone)

On Armistice Day, 11 November 1920, the body of the Unknown Soldier was taken on a gun carriage and interred under a black marble slab in Westminster Abbey. The inscription reads:

'Beneath this stone rests the body of a British warrior, unknown by name or rank, brought from France to lie among the most illustrious of the land and buried here on Armistice Day 11 November 1920, in the presence of His Majesty King George V, his Ministers of State, the Chiefs of the Forces and a vast concourse of the nation.'

The King also unveiled a permanent Cenotaph to replace the temporary one used the year before and at 11 o'clock, as requested by his Majesty, silence fell over the vast crowds who stood with bowed heads for two minutes remembering the fallen, a respectful tradition that continues to this day.

Post-war Britain suffered many economic, political and social problems in the years following the war and getting back to normal was by no means an easy option. By 1922 one in five of the working population was actively seeking work and in towns and cities it was a common sight to see young men with limbs missing and terrible injuries begging on streets.

In the countryside families who had lived on the estates for hundreds of years were finding themselves unable to afford their

Group of men at Prees Heath Camp (courtesy of Peter Lea)

upkeep. With large numbers of country houses being sold off as high taxation and death duties took their toll, along with their demise went the employment they had provided over the centuries. Work was increasingly hard to find and much bad feeling was felt against women who sought to retain their jobs.

A boom in births occurred between 1918 and 1920 with an increase of forty-five per cent in the population recorded. Understandably this led to the need for more housing; both Oswestry and Whitchurch were regularly discussing this issue in local council meetings as they tried to carry out Lloyd George's promise of a 'land fit for heroes to live in'.

It wouldn't be until 1920 that medals for those who had fought throughout World War One were awarded to the survivors. The 1914-15 Star, the 1918 British War Medal, and the Allied Victory Medal soon became known by their recipients as Pip, Squeak and Wilfred, named after *Daily Mirror* strip cartoon characters of the time. The sense of humour needed to survive four long years of war was still present.

And as the years passed memories of the appalling upheaval caused by a devastating world war began to take a back seat to the day to day

Group of men at Prees Heath Camp (courtesy of Peter Lea)

task of living. Certainly no one could have comprehended as life returned to normal in Oswestry, Whitchurch and their surrounding boroughs that in just twenty-one years time the country would once again be drawn into a devastating war.

Battlefields
Empty and wide the fields
Sweep to the horizon
Tranquil and untroubled

Nothing remains
Of the blood spilt, lives lost
Only the wind sighs.

Remembering
Remembering
The fallen.

Bibliography

The majority of information for this book was sourced from the 1913-19 files of the *Oswestry & Border Counties Advertizer* and the *Whitchurch Herald* newspapers held on microfilm in the town's libraries.

A wide range of books and websites were consulted to verify the accuracy of the general information used, a brief selection of which follows:

The Great War 1914-18, SSAFA's Official Guide to World War 1
Home Front 1914-1918 by Ian F.W. Beckett, National Archives
Fighting on the Home Front by Kate Adie, Hodder
A Short History of the First World War by Gordon Kerr, Pocket Essentials
Kelly's Directory, 1913
www.iwm.org.uk/history/first-world-war
http://newspapers.library.wales/
www.britishnewspaperarchive.co.uk
www.historylearningsite.co.uk
www.greatwar.co.uk
https://en.wikipedia.org
http://search.shropshirehistory.org.uk
www.oswestrygenealogy.org.uk
www.whitchurch-heritage.co.uk

Index

Aliens, 33, 41, 153
Archbishop of Canterbury, 115
Armistice and the Peace Treaty, 142, 168
Asquith, Herbert Henry, 26, 65

Bailleul, Rainald de, 10
Battle of Ancre, 109
Battle of Arras, 119
Battle of Loos, 65, 132
Battle of Mons, 26
Battle of the Somme, 84, 86, 106
Battle of Ypres (Second), 65, 84, 86–7
Black Hand Movement, 23
Bridgman, Viscount W.C. MP, 38, 149
British Summer Time Act, 84, 103–4

Cabrinovic, Nedeljko, 23
Campbell OBE VC, Lt Col J.V., 134–5
Cannock Chase German War Cemetery, 54
Capel, Lord, 16–17
Cavell, Edith, 66
Cenotaph, 157, 168
Churchill, Winston, 66
Conscientious Objectors, 26, 83
Corrie, Maj Wynne, 48, 159

Cromwell, Oliver, 10, 13

Defence of the Realm Act (DORA), 25, 42, 68, 98, 101, 103
Drunkenness, 45, 65, 115

Ellesmere Canal, 17, 21–2, 99
Entertainment:
  bands, 36, 97, 101
  cinemas, 59, 73, 76, 119
  circuses, 72, 81, 145, 152
  concerts, 40, 75, 78, 101
  dances, 68, 89, 145, 157
  fetes and sports days, 98–9, 105, 152, 117–18
  pantomimes, 75, 110, 121

Ferdinand, Archduke Franz, 23
Folkestone and London bombardment (1917), 109–10

George, Lloyd, 65, 84, 106, 109, 169
German, Edward, 102, 122
Godsal family, Iscoyd Park, 39, 131
Great Western Railway, 16, 131, 136
Great Yarmouth and King's Lynn bombardment (1915), 64, 84

INDEX

Hanmer, Maj Wyndham, 43, 78
Harlech, Lord and Lady, 14, 32, 36, 116, 143, 146
Harper Adams Agricultural College, 69
Hartlepool, Scarborough and Whitby shelling (1914), 28, 30
Hesperian, RMS, 81
Holbache, David, 10

Influenza (Spanish Flu), 62, 155–6

King Edward I, 16
King George V, 65–6, 140, 157
King Oswald of Northumbria, 10
King Penda of Mercia, 10
King William the Conqueror, 10, 16
King's Shropshire Light Infantry (KSLI), 42, 75, 119
Kitchener, FM H., 26, 78, 84

London and North Western Railway, 58, 136
Lusitania, RMS, 65, 70

Maycock, Pte, 53–4
Medals and the men who deserved them:
  Croix de Guerre, 129
  Distinguished Conduct Medal, 129–30
  Distinguished Flying Cross, 130
  Distinguished Service Cross, 130–1
  Distinguished Service Order, 131, 135
  Meritorious Service Medal, 132
  Military Cross, 132–3, 139
  Military Medal, 130, 133–4
  Pip, Squeak and Wilfred, 169
  Victoria Cross, 134–6
Montgomery, Roger de, 10

Neutrality League, 26

Oster, Willie, 53–4
Oswestry:
  Ardmillan Auxiliary Hospital, 74, 90, 145, 149
  Bailey Head, 13, 16, 35, 73
  Baird, J. & R., Tailors and Outfitters, 68
  Beckitt and Sons, Grocers, 111, 118
  Bradley & Co, Drapers, 111, 113, 148–9
  Brogyntyn Hall, 14, 117
  Cae Glas Park, 14, 33, 71, 147, 160
  Caer Ogyrfan Iron Age Hillfort, 10, 137
  Cambrian Engine and Railway, 13, 16, 112, 116, 162
  Christ Church, 36
  Cross Market, 16
  Dales Brothers Emporium, 68
  Guildhall, 13, 32, 35, 94, 116, 159
  Higham, G.G., Gunmaker, 112

Hobley's Tea Rooms, 38, 74
King's Theatre, 110, 121
Memorial Hall, 36, 159
Messrs H. Jones & Son, Oil Dealers, 31
Powis Market Hall, 16, 149
Presbyterian Church, 90
Schools, 10, 14, 36
Smales Almshouses, 14
St Oswald's Parish Church, 68, 94, 148, 160
Thomas, W.H. & Sons, 72
Victoria Assembly Rooms, 36, 89, 157
Oswestry and Border Counties Advertizer, 14, 31, 90, 96, 98
Owen, Wilfred, 136–9

Pacifists, 125–6
PALS, 28, 33, 68
Park Hall Camp, 31, 47–56, 69, 71, 149, 154
Prees Heath Camp, 43, 56–63, 125, 154, 156
Princess Mary, 44
Princip, Gavro, 24

Queen Elizabeth I, 10

Rationing, 128, 140, 142–3, 160, 166
Red Cross, 28, 36, 38, 73, 80
Refugees, 31, 35, 41, 63, 159
Robert Jones and Agnes Hunt Hospital, Oswestry, 55
Robinson VC, Lt Leefe and the SL11 German airship, 84–6

Shortages of:
  Food, 84, 87, 108, 122, 142–3
  Other essentials, 107, 111–12, 120–1, 124
Shrewsbury and Chester Railway, 16
Shropshire Union Canal, 99, 147
Silvertown Munitions Factory disaster (1917), 108
Stanier, Capt Beville MP, 81, 152

Tanks, 86, 109, 130, 135
Teck, Duchess of, 105
Thankful villages, 155
Tomb of the Unknown Soldier, 168
Treaty of London (1839), 24
Tribunals, 96, 104, 107, 109, 115, 127
Tsar Nicholas II and the Russian Royal family, 140

U-boats, 131, 152

Vendome, Duchess of, Belgium, 41

War Memorials, 62, 160, 162, 164, 166
Warenne William de, 16
Wem, 17
Whitchurch:
  Album Monasterium (White Church), 16
  Almshouses, 14, 20

INDEX 175

Broughall Auxiliary Hospital, 41, 75, 106, 150, 167
Brownlow Street, 19, 151
Dodington, 20, 102
Egerton Drill Hall, 19, 39, 43, 78
Green End, 19, 39, 78–9
Joyce, J.B., turret clock mfg, 21
Jubilee Park, 19, 104, 123, 151
Mediolanum, 16
Melton Lodge, 19
Norton, E.P., Cheese Factor, 39
Schools, 19, 41, 127, 164
Sherryman's Bridge, 17
Smith, W.H. & Co, Engineers, 20, 39, 78, 80
St Alkmund's Church, 20, 60, 76, 154
Town Hall, 19, 39, 80, 105, 164
Watergate Street, 80, 106
West Farmstead (Westune), 16
Wyatt Brothers, heating eqpt, 20
Whitchurch Herald, 19, 42, 101–102, 105, 123, 150

Whitfield VC, Sgt Harold, 135–6
Whittington, 50
Wilson, President Woodrow, 109
Women's occupations during and after the war:
after the war, 142, 159–60, 167, 169
League of Honour, 44
munitions, 28, 110
National Union of Women Workers (NUWW), 156–7
police officers, 28, 69, 151
Voluntary Aid Detachment (VAD), 28, 74, 99
women on the land, 69, 90, 98, 128, 152
Women's Army Auxiliary Corp (WAAC), 121
Women's Royal Air Force (WRAF), 146

YMCA, 50–1, 59–60, 71, 145

Zeppelins, 64–5, 90, 105, 110, 140